Retirement Compass

Personal Finance for the Life You Desire

EMILY MACPHERSON

RETHINK PRESS

TABLE OF CONTENTS

*I dedicate this book to my mum and dad
who have always shown me
unwavering love and encouragement.*

INTRODUCTION

A hundred years ago, the modern concept of retirement didn't really exist. Most people would have expected to work until they died, or if they were lucky, to be supported in later life by their children. Even 50 years ago, retirement might have meant about five to ten years of a quiet life before they died.

Today, most people aim to stop work sometime between their mid-fifties and their early seventies. They are generally in reasonable health when they retire and expect to spend at least 15 to 20 active years doing all the things they didn't have time for while they were at work.

This of course requires money.

Managing money is a necessary part of planning for retirement, but the banking crisis, miss-selling scandals and misaligned motives of the financial services industry have led us to fall out of love with our personal finances. At the same time, modern day society encourages us to drive for bigger, better, more, and to judge ourselves and others on our material possessions and apparent financial success.

Rather than seeing our finances as a mechanism for achieving the lifestyle we desire, we tend to view them as a means to pursue social ideals. We have become disconnected from our personal finances, and our personal finances have become disconnected from what is important to us as individuals.

The purpose of this book is to guide you in reconnecting with what is truly important to you. It will assist you in identifying your highest values and provide you with an understanding of how you can plan your retirement with those values at the core.

As a Chartered Financial Planner with over 15 years' experience assisting clients to plan for retirement, I am conscious of the dilemmas we face when considering making the retirement leap. These include:

- ⊙ Knowing how much is 'enough', and how you will know when you have it

- ⊙ Indecision – fear of making the leap

- ⊙ A lack of direction or focus

- ⊙ Aches and pains and health concerns (yours and those of the people around you)

- ⊙ Concerns over missed opportunities and fear that there is 'no going back'

- ⊙ Worry over the direction of wider society.

Retirement Compass aims to adjust your perspective so that you are able to approach retirement with a different outlook. Exploring the bigger picture will provide you with the foundations from which to build your individual financial plan.

I chose financial planning as a career in response to an uneasy first experience as a client of the industry. Fed up with the way the adviser had made me feel, I wanted to do a better job than he had. I have come to realise that the most critical part of any financial plan is the meaning behind it. You can crunch the numbers to maximise returns, minimise costs and reduce tax, all you like, but it doesn't mean anything if you are not living the life you want to lead.

As you discover how to use your financial resources as a mechanism for living in alignment with your highest values, the possibilities become more exciting and the myriad of choices easier to navigate.

The first part of this book tells the story of my journey into the world of financial services. I share my experiences, mistakes and insights, as well as the realisations that have shaped my beliefs and sparked my determination to make a positive change.

The second part will provide you with a summary of the main financial options to consider as you plan for your retirement. It is not designed to make you a financial expert, or to provide you with all the technical information you will need to structure your finances exactly. The basic level of qualification required to become a financial adviser includes a programme of six study units which take an average of 370 hours to complete. To cover all the combinations of options in sufficient detail to enable you to identify which solutions are right for you would take textbooks full of technical information, which would probably be out of date by the time you'd finished reading them. Furthermore, my whole approach demands that all this technical detail needs to be adapted and tailored to your individual requirements. This cannot be achieved in a book.

My intention is that after reading this book, you will have a clear and inspiring foundation from which to build your personal retirement plan, but it is not a substitute for professional financial advice. Whether you enlist the services of a professional to assist you in organising the technical details of your finances is for you to decide, but I believe that, when done properly, financial planning has the power to change lives for the better.

The vision of my company, Find Peace of Mind, is to enhance levels of wellbeing in society by transforming people's relationships with their finances. This book is part of realising that vision. I hope you enjoy it and that it fulfils its purpose.

PART 1

THE REAL
FINANCIAL CRISIS

CHAPTER 1

The Beginning

The adviser in the pinstriped suit

It was the summer of 2002 and all was well with the world. I had just achieved a first in my business degree and secured a sought-after place on a graduate trainee scheme at a leading actuarial consultancy.

Having seen me and my brother through university, my mum and dad had chosen to up sticks from our family home in Fleet, Hampshire and move to Somerset where my mum grew up. At the same time, my boyfriend Colin and I decided to take the plunge, pool our resources, and buy our first house.

It was with a mixture of excitement and trepidation that I prepared my parents' sitting room for our first meeting with financial adviser, Tristan Till. He had visited my parents at the house before, but I wanted to make a good impression. We had found our dream house – well actually, it was a complete wreck, but it had the potential to be exactly what we wanted, and we hoped we could afford it.

Tristan pulled up outside in his sparkling Audi and walked up the drive. My excitement about the start of our 'grown up' future was bubbling nicely. As I took Tristan's coat, a strong waft of aftershave filled the air. He was very well presented in a dark blue pinstriped suit and crisp light blue shirt. His greying hair was neatly trimmed, he was clean shaven and his smart leather briefcase and polished black shoes oozed financial professionalism.

As we sat down and discussed our situation, Tristan explained that securing a mortgage wasn't necessarily as straightforward as we had first thought. Because I hadn't yet started my job, we would need to apply for what was known as a self-certification mortgage. This involved an application where the mortgage lender would not require any proof of income; instead, we could just state our income on the form and they would agree to lend without wanting to see payslips, which of course I didn't yet have. Despite the need to self-certify, Tristan reassured us, as long as we passed the credit check and the survey on the property was acceptable, the mortgage would be ours.

Tristan agreed to prepare the paperwork which we received a few days later. Initially I thought he had made a mistake because he had put my income down as zero and inflated my boyfriend's income to almost double what it should have been.

I was left feeling stupid as I put down the phone to Tristan, having called him to let him know about the apparent error. He explained that this was the way it needed to be to get the mortgage. The mortgage company just wanted to know the overall income figure and I shouldn't worry about it as he had it all sorted.

OK, I thought. It didn't feel quite right, but who was I to question the adviser in the pinstriped suit?

I asked my dad to look over the paperwork and it turned out that the mortgage Tristan had recommended for us was the same as the mortgage he had organised for my parents. My dad ran his own company, and Tristan had explained that this meant a self-certification mortgage was necessary for them too. It was a striking coincidence, given the vast number of mortgages available, that this particular mortgage product would be the one that suited both us and my parents best.

As matters progressed I became increasingly baffled about the process of securing the mortgage and the insurance products we needed to run alongside it. I'm the sort of person who likes to understand things, but after a while I felt like I shouldn't ask any more questions. Most of those I had asked seemed to have been brushed aside rather than addressed by Tristan. Still, I thought he must know best.

We had discussed life insurance and agreed that we wanted to be sure that the mortgage would be repaid should either of us die. We also needed some protection in case either of us suffered a critical illness, but both Colin and I had comprehensive sick pay and long term income protection through our employers, so we explained that we didn't need any extra income protection cover.

When the insurance paperwork came through, income protection cover had been included and Tristan was very reluctant to remove it. When he eventually did arrange for the income protection insurance to be removed, I noticed that the commission he was due to receive had dropped by over £500.

Ultimately, we got the mortgage we needed to buy the cottage we had set our hearts on, but as the process unfolded, I became increasingly uncomfortable with Tristan's approach. I didn't really understand the products we had been sold, or whether everything had been done entirely above board. My discomfort was fuelled by the fact that, as the sale of my parents' house fell through, Tristan was caught out trying to cheat the system.

He'd advised my parents to apply for an additional mortgage, secured on their house in Fleet. This would enable them to raise a deposit to put down on the Somerset property without the need to sell straight away. Grateful to find a solution rather than lose their dream home, my parents had agreed to the second mortgage, which was again an exact replica of the mortgage both they and I had already been sold.

Unbeknown to my parents, Tristan had submitted each mortgage application on the basis that the mortgage in question was going to be the only one they held. The first they knew of this was when the mortgage company alerted them to the issue by threatening to cancel both applications. The solution Tristan had recommended wasn't allowed, and his recommendation almost cost my parents the house they had set their hearts on.

Thankfully my parents found another buyer who was able to act quickly and they made the move to Somerset. We were able to move into our cottage in the August, providing me with a few weeks of dedicated DIY before I started work.

Knowing what I know now, I realise there was no need for either me or my parents to have a self-certification mortgage. I could have provided a contract of employment and my dad tax returns or accounts, and we would have saved a few pounds a month by applying to a different lender and supplying proof of our income. The self-certification lender did, however, pay 0.15% more commission to Tristan.

The M25 commute

It's often said that even accountants find actuaries boring, but the work on my graduate trainee scheme was right up my street. Maths was my favourite subject at school and I have always been one of those strange people who gets excited by figures and spreadsheets. I was happy to undertake the tasks required of me and was able to fulfil my quota of 'chargeable hours' on client projects comfortably.

I worked within the insurance department which provided consultancy to insurance companies. Our projects included tasks such as assessing claims statistics, identifying trends in longevity, and using complex models to assess how the insurers should price their policies, to name but a few. On an individual level I got on well with my colleagues and formed some good friendships, but there was something that didn't sit quite right with me about the collective corporate culture.

I was in a different position to most of the other graduates on my trainee scheme because I already had a long term partner and, having bought our project house, we had DIY to occupy us at evenings and weekends. Most of the other graduates lived fairly close to the office in Reigate, but I had a 40-mile commute around the M25 to get to work each morning and evening, taking just over an hour on a good day. I tended to get to work fairly early to avoid the traffic, but I was keen to leave for home as close to five as possible. In my lunch break I would either eat lunch at my desk, to ensure I could get home without delay, or I would take a short wander into town if I needed to pick anything up.

After six months or so of the M25 commute, I started to worry that a career as an actuary wasn't for me. The work was enjoyable, but I didn't find it particularly meaningful because, in the business to business environment, I couldn't see a direct impact on real people.

I reached crisis point after my first appraisal during which my line manager praised me for the quality of my work, but explained that if I wanted to progress my career I would need to come out with my colleagues for evening drinks, eat lunch in the canteen and get myself noticed by the partners. This really wasn't me. I am confident in myself, my ideas and my abilities, but I have never been one to put on a show or be someone I'm not. I'm an introvert by nature, and tying to 'put myself out there' makes me feel awkward. Even now I shy away from things like networking events, and I am much more comfortable being in the background than being the centre of attention, either in a business or a social setting.

The evening after my appraisal, I found myself making an unplanned trip to Somerset to seek the advice of my mum and dad. Should I give up a well-paid job and the defined career path that I had worked so hard to secure just because it didn't feel like me?

I think I already knew the answer, and that my parents would support me in it, but I needed to hear them say it. One of the lasting messages I recall from childhood discussions with my parents is 'You can do anything you want to do if you put your mind to it'. However, I had genuinely thought that a career as an actuary was what I wanted, and this made it all the more difficult to accept that I had made a mistake.

My parents' support was unwavering. Even though I had no idea what I actually wanted to do, I made the decision to resign my place on the graduate trainee scheme and seek fulfilment elsewhere.

I didn't leave straight away and my employers were fantastic. When I explained my predicament to my boss, he offered me the option of transferring to another area within the company, and the firm also arranged for me to attend an external career strategy session. I didn't transfer, and the strategy session disappointingly suggested I would be best suited to being an actuary or an accountant, but my employers kindly kept me on for an extended notice period while I worked out where my career was heading.

During my time on the trainee scheme I had worked within the strategy team. A project that had particularly sparked my interest was one that looked at the role of Independent Financial Advisers as distributors of financial services products. It took me back to the sinking feeling I associated with Tristan Till and reinforced the message that a financial adviser's primary objective is to sell (or distribute) financial products rather than give genuine advice. This was a very different concept to my naïve mental picture of a caring adviser working hard to better the lives of his clients. I felt let down by the reality, but at the same time determined to try to change things; to be the one to deliver the caring, genuine service I had expected to be the norm.

I decided to pursue a career as an Independent Financial Adviser (IFA), doing things my way – the perfect combination of relationships and figures and the ability to have a positive impact on people's lives. I wrote a letter to a small firm of financial advisers within cycling distance of my house, and they agreed to take me on as an administrator while I self-studied for the prerequisite IFA qualifications.

From the off I felt much more like me. Maybe it was the fact that the job was closer to home, or the fact that there were only four of us in the company so there was no chance of the three Directors not knowing who I was, even if I didn't eat lunch with them every day. It might have been that I was doing something where I was able to see the positive influence I could have on people's lives directly. Most likely, it was a combination of all these factors. I had taken a 45% pay cut, but I was happy, and once again excited about what the future had in store.

CHAPTER 2

Products, Panels And Pay

Products

One of the first things I learned in my new role was the importance of 'disclosure'. The industry regulator at the time, the Financial Services Authority (FSA), insisted that when meeting a client, a financial adviser must provide them with a document outlining the type of service being offered. Every firm used a template, setting out each type of financial product (mortgages, investments, insurance) with a tick box to indicate whether the firm provided independent advice in relation to that type of product or was tied to a certain product provider. The idea was that the standardised approach made it easier for clients to see what type of advice they were getting.

My key gripe with this approach is that it immediately channels the discussion towards products, when in fact the client might not need a financial product at all. The focus should be on the right advice. We are now at a point where people generally only pick up the phone to a financial adviser if they think they need a financial product, and that definitely doesn't fit with my model.

The 'tick box' product sales approach to disclosure remains the norm, and only recently has the regulator, now the Financial Conduct Authority (FCA), begun to consider it may not be appropriate. Every six months, financial advisory firms must send a report to the regulator confirming that they are profitable, appropriately insured and hold sufficient cash in the bank. Any complaints must be categorised by the product to which they relate, income is broken down by product type, and regulatory fees are allocated depending on the volume of business a firm achieves for each product line.

I struggle to reconcile this every time I submit my report – in my little world, advice means advice, not product sales.

The definition of independence in relation to financial advice has changed over the years I have been involved in the industry. Currently, to be independent, an adviser must consider the full range of financial products across the 'whole of the market'. If they only consider products from a restricted range of product types or providers, they are offering restricted advice.

In theory this makes sense, but the complication comes in the definitions. For example, while I was learning the ropes at the small local firm, a concept that struck me as odd was the 'whole of market mortgage panel'. I had expected the term 'whole of market' to mean exactly that. In the context of mortgage advice, I would expect it to mean that the adviser was considering the full range of mortgage products from the full range of mortgage providers.

Little did I know.

Panels

It transpired that a panel comprised a select number of products from a limited range of providers, and the idea was that advisers picked products from that select group. When I started providing mortgage advice, I was asked to work from a 'whole of market mortgage panel' consisting of around 10 mortgage lenders – less than 10% of the total number of lenders offering mortgages at the time.

I remember questioning the concept with one of the Directors of the firm. He explained that the panel had been put together to represent the whole of the market, so there was one lender which specialised in self-certification mortgages, one which specialised in mortgages on investment properties, one which specialised in loans to people with adverse credit, and so on. I couldn't quite get my head around it, particularly when I became qualified to give advice and started to research the available products for individual clients.

The first client I recommended a mortgage to was a kind gentleman whom I had come to know while we were walking our dogs in the park. He was aware that I was now giving advice and asked me if I would review his mortgage for him because his monthly payment had just gone up.

I did my research, sourcing mortgages from the (actual) whole of the market, and identified the product that could meet my client's requirements most cost effectively. Being new to the process, I was required to have any advice I gave signed off by one of the Directors and I welcomed the second opinion, wanting to make absolutely sure this gentleman was getting the best deal. The Director told me that the product I had identified wasn't on the panel so I needed to find an alternative that was. The trouble with that was the best 'on panel' alternative would cost my friend an extra £50 a month because of the higher interest rate.

I queried this with my boss and he explained that we would get 'struck off' the panel for not using it. When I questioned what would happen if we got 'struck off', he explained that we would lose the preferential commission rates being paid to the 'whole of market panel' members. It all became clear and my heart sank.

I thought of my dog walking acquaintance and I couldn't justify recommending the 'on panel' solution. I did a bit more digging and found out that it was permissible for the firm as a whole to recommend a small proportion of business 'off panel', and I convinced my boss to allow me to recommend the cheaper solution. At the same time, I knew I couldn't work like this for long so I started to think about setting up on my own.

Pay

Once I had passed my exams and gained some experience in an administrative role, it was time for me to negotiate a package as a fully-fledged adviser. The standard approach was for an adviser to be self-employed and earn a set percentage of any income they generated for the company. We settled on a sixty-forty split in my favour, and I was happy with that until the company recruited a new adviser on a seventy-thirty split. I had been generating a steady stream of business and was building up referrals so I was disappointed that my efforts hadn't been recognised.

It wasn't until I'd handed in my notice that the Directors offered me an equal package, but by then it was too late. I was grateful to the firm for giving me the experience I needed, but what I had learned about industry practices hadn't all been good. The reason I had chosen to pursue a career in financial advice was because of my uncomfortable experience with the adviser in the pinstriped suit. I knew the reality of working in the industry wouldn't fit perfectly with the way I thought things should be, but I hadn't realised how systemic the issues were.

It was generally accepted that in order to increase sales of a particular product, insurance companies and other financial services providers just needed to increase the level of commission they paid to advisers for selling that product. The whole of market panel typified the problem, and what scared me the most was that I felt like the odd one out for questioning it.

I have always been a person of strong moral principles. I will shoot myself in the foot rather than compromise those principles. As an example, a couple of years ago I was out with the girls at a Thai restaurant. The food had been great and the service likewise. We were the last to leave the restaurant, and when we were presented with the bill, we realised it was much less than we had anticipated. The waiter hadn't charged us for any of the wine – and there had been a few bottles!

We had hushed exchanges across the table while we worked out what mistake had been made. I prompted a brief debate about raising it with the waiter, but the rest of the girls dismissed my suggestion and we all laughed about my discomfort at accepting the error in our favour. They know if I had been there on my own, I would have confessed the undercharge without a thought, but I couldn't be responsible for all of them having to pay more just because of my morals. So we paid the bill and left, with me making sure not to catch the eye of the waiter for fear of giving us away.

This type of moral conflict seemed inevitable within my chosen career. It was not only the level of commission on products that worried me, but the fact that pay was contingent with a product sale.

Early on in my advisory career, Simon approached me to request a review of his pension. He had built up two separate pension pots over the years, one valued at £100,000 and the second worth £50,000. He had recently started his own business and wanted to transfer his old pensions to a new arrangement and re-start contributions. His objective was to have a clearer view of exactly what his pensions were worth so that we could manage them more effectively to maximise their value and ultimately enhance his income in retirement.

Without going into the technical detail, I identified that there was a slight disadvantage to transferring the larger of the two old pensions. However, I would only get paid if the transfer went ahead, since it was the commission payable by the new pension provider in return for receiving the £100,000 transfer value that would cover the cost of my research.

When I found myself going round in circles trying to justify the transfer, I had to have a word with myself. The right answer was clear. The transfer was everything I stood against, and the fact that I was even considering it was testament to the fact that there was something very wrong with the industry.

I realised I wasn't going to be able to work within the confines imposed on me by my employers. Within two years of setting out on a defined career path in a stable industry, I found myself sitting in a makeshift office at the back of my garage with no clients or start-up capital, wondering how on earth I was going to change the world of financial advice.

CHAPTER 3

The Hostile Takeover

Retail Distribution Review

Somehow, I made things work and became a well-established self-employed IFA doing things my way. In 2005 I set up Find Peace of Mind Limited Liability Partnership, which later incorporated as Find Peace of Mind Limited.

Having fallen in love with rural Somerset, Colin and I followed my parents to the West Country in 2006 and had our first child in 2007. All the while I continued to enjoy my work assisting clients with their financial planning, through the credit crunch and beyond.

After having my second child in 2010, I decided that I needed some support in the business. I had subcontracted administrative duties to a number of self-employed friends and family members in the past, but if I'm honest, none of these arrangements had really worked out for either party. Now was the time to take on a real employee: someone I didn't have an existing arrangement with who had the skills, ambition and experience to support me initially in keeping the business ticking over, and in the future help to develop it into one which could make a difference in more people's lives.

I am extremely lucky to have found Neil. Disillusioned having spent 30 years in the world of banking and fed up with commuting for hours every day, he was looking for a change in lifestyle and direction and agreed to come to work for me on half his previous pay. He was even prepared to share the office with our two dogs!

It was Neil who, in late 2011, spotted an advert in the local paper for a qualified IFA placed by a businessman called Tim Green. Tim was in his late 60s and had been a financial adviser for over 30 years, having built up a large client bank in the area. I didn't ask Neil why he was looking in the job ads section of the paper, but seeing as that was over five years ago and he is still here, I'm confident it was in the interest of the company!

Neil didn't know Tim but, having grown up in the same locality, he was vaguely aware of his history and connections. He correctly predicted that Tim was advertising for a qualified adviser to work within his company because regulatory changes meant he would imminently be in a position where he was no longer able to give advice.

In 2012 came the Retail Distribution Review (RDR). This was a review of the way financial products were distributed, and two of the key outcomes for us IFAs were the abolition of commission from investment and pension products and the need to achieve a higher level of adviser qualification than had previously been the case. Interestingly, advisers who are not independent, for example bank staff, can still be paid by means of commission.

For me the changes in regulation were largely immaterial. By this time I had naturally shifted to a fee based charging model, agreeing fees with clients that were not influenced by any product sale. Although the new regulations didn't go so far as to detach pay from product completely, at least they forced the discussion around fees for everyone. I had also continued my process of self-study and had already achieved the new prerequisite Level 4 diploma status. When the RDR rules came in on 1 January

2012, however, many advisers found themselves unable to give advice, and Tim was one of these advisers.

Mr Timothy Green

Our first meeting with Tim was in the lounge of an historic local hotel where he had connections. There was a vague sense of déjà vu as Tim greeted me with a firm handshake, a waft of aftershave, and a blue pinstriped suit.

I felt slightly in awe of this gentleman as he explained how he had built up a successful business over 30+ years, generating enough renewal income (that is regular income from policies already in place) to cover the salary of a decent employee. He was well-known in the community, having links with local property developers, estate agents and solicitors.

Tim explained how he had hoped to retire a year or so ago, but when he tried to sell his client bank to another firm, it had not delivered the service he'd expected, forcing him back to work. He was looking for an exit route, but one which ensured that his clients were properly cared for.

We seemed to be on the same wavelength.

Although it was my company proposing to take over his, his air of confidence made it easy to forget that. It seemed like a fantastic opportunity and time was of the essence. To make it work, we only had a couple of months before the new regulations came in.

If it hadn't been for my dad, who insisted on drawing up a sale and purchase agreement between the companies, I would have naively (and stupidly) gone into it on blind trust. Thankfully, he put together a contract which we would later come to rely on.

We agreed to buy Tim's client bank for an initial sum, with a further sum payable after 90% of his clients had successfully transferred across. In addition to the lump sums, Tim would receive 60% of all renewal income from his old client bank over a three-year period, with us delivering the ongoing support to those clients. During those three years, Tim would work with us as a relationship manager to ensure that his clients were happily transitioned to my company and to introduce us to any new clients who approached him through his network of connections. New introductions would earn Tim 20% of the income they generated for the company.

It seemed like a win-win. Tim's clients were appropriately serviced, he had a way out and we had a growth opportunity. We knew there would be lots to do, but we set off on our new venture with excitement and optimism.

The cracks began to appear fairly soon after the contract was signed. Neil and I were still working from my converted garage (with the dogs), but Tim operated from a grand office in a nearby city. He was adamant that a central office was a necessity, and while I didn't disagree that it would be useful for meeting clients, the significant cost seemed hard to justify.

Eventually we settled on a smaller office in the same building at a much reduced cost, a compromise for which I was never really forgiven. Although image and grandeur were the primary motivators, another key reason Tim battled for a large office was the sheer volume of client files he needed to store. Any financial adviser is required to hold copies of client records for a number of years after giving advice. I'm not sure I can accurately describe our office as paperless, but we do store everything electronically. Tim's approach, on the other hand, was definitely paper based. In addition to the grandeur of the office, the price we were prepared to pay for his armoury of filing cabinets was a point of contention during our initial discussions. There were also a number of other seemingly small disconnects that in hindsight should have set alarm bells ringing.

As time went by, the relationship deteriorated. The renewal income didn't materialise at anywhere near the level Tim had promised, yet he still expected us to pay his second lump sum. He had a handwritten list of clients and policies he claimed had transferred to my company, along with a scribbled note next to each stating the renewal income we should now be receiving. Our electronic records and the physical payments painted a completely different picture.

When an insurance policy is set up, the adviser typically receives a lump sum of initial commission. Then, after a period of usually around four years, the adviser receives further much smaller 'renewal' payments. The idea is that these smaller payments cover the adviser's time in servicing the policy. Insurance policies aren't affected by the RDR commission ban so they still work in this way.

For example, for setting up a policy with premiums of £25 per month, an adviser might receive an initial commission of £1,000, then 50p a month from year four onwards. There is a delay before the smaller renewal payments because the 'initial earnings period' is when the cost of paying the initial commission is recouped by the provider. If a client cancels the policy during this initial earnings period, the provider will claw back a proportion of the commission from the adviser.

It transpired that a significant proportion of the renewal income Tim had on his list was in respect of policies he had only just put in place, and no income was due to be paid on these policies for another four years. We were therefore committing to looking after these clients for that period without anything in return. More alarmingly, some of the policies Tim had put in place were being cancelled by clients, resulting in us having to cover claw backs of initial commission that we had never actually received in the first place.

I still believed that this man must know better than me; he had so much more experience and apparent success.

I remember on one occasion going with Tim to visit an elderly couple whose investment portfolio he had looked after for many years. Tim pulled me up before we left the office because I hadn't packed the three lever arch files of paperwork to take with me.

'You must take the files,' he warned. 'It gives them confidence that you have done lots of work for them to see all the paper.'

During the meeting, we discussed the clients' requirements, and I followed up with a report and some suggestions for reorganising their portfolio to make cost reductions and tax savings. This in itself was slightly awkward since I was effectively undermining the structure that Tim had put in place.

I got a call from the clients' son Richard asking me how much I was going to make in commission as a result of the restructure. I had been warned about Richard by Tim who had described him as awkward, and although Tim had also advised him in the past, there was a suggestion of a recent feud. I explained to Richard that it was not possible to take a commission from investment policies any more so I was making no charge for the restructure. To me this was part of getting to know the clients so that I could continue to assist them moving forward. I explained that we were already receiving renewal income from the investments agreed by his father and this covered the cost of the ongoing service.

Not long afterwards Richard contacted me to arrange a meeting with him and his parents. I attended alone and with slight trepidation since he had seemed very cagey and somewhat aggressive during my two telephone discussions with him.

I arrived at the appointment and was greeted warmly by the elderly couple, and we chatted through my proposals which were received positively. When Richard joined us, the atmosphere changed abruptly. He launched into what I can only describe as a verbal assault, expressing his contempt at how my company had gone behind his back to transfer his policies under our control without his consent and how he wanted all the commission we had received from those policies paid back.

Although I hadn't expected the meeting to be plain sailing, I was taken aback at the level of anger Richard clearly felt and the distrust and aggression he directed at me. I have never felt so intimidated in a professional situation, but as I sat and took Richard's verbal battering, I could understand his frustrations.

I was shocked to hear that Richard had expressly told Tim that he did not want his policies, or those of his wife, transferred across to Find Peace of Mind. Tim had, through a backdoor process known as novation, gone ahead and made the transfer anyway. Richard's request not to transfer had been made before I had had any dealings with the family and it was Tim's authority upon which the policies had been transferred, so I knew that I had done nothing wrong.

It transpired there had been bad blood between Richard and Tim for some years. I never quite got to the bottom of what had happened, but it was clear that any trust Richard had ever had in financial advisers had been well and truly broken.

I listened to what Richard had to say, maintained my
professionalism and apologised that his policies had been
transferred without his consent, explaining that I had not been
aware of his request not to transfer. Before he would allow me
to leave the house, he forced me to provide him with a written
agreement that I would repay any income we had received since
his policies had been transferred to our company. I was actually
in agreement with most of the points Richard made and I would
have refunded him the commission whether he had forced me
to or not. What I didn't agree with was the way he treated me,
and as I arranged for the refund to be processed that afternoon,
I was pleased to cut ties with someone who had made me feel
sick to the stomach about the profession I had chosen and
people's perceptions of me as a result.

I relayed the story to Neil, who told me how Tim had recently
mentioned taking a client to court for cancelling an insurance
policy that had cost him £10,000 in clawed back commission.
The panic set in. How could he ever justify taking commission
at that level, let alone sue the client for cancelling his own policy
because he had had to pay some of the commission back? The
alarm bells ringing in my head were now at such a level that they
were impossible to ignore.

We then discovered that, despite having been set up with a company
e-mail address and telephone system, Tim was e-mailing existing
and potential clients from a separate account, providing them with
personal contact details and purporting to give advice in his own
name even though he was not qualified to do so.

After numerous uncomfortable disciplinary meetings, I came
to the realisation that this nearly 70-year-old member of the 'old
boys club' was never going to be told what to do by a woman in

her mid-30s. Even when he promised to change his ways so that he would be allowed to continue introducing business and therefore earning income, it didn't take long before I realised he had done no such thing. Importantly, I also realised that he didn't actually know better than me and I needed to be stronger in my belief that I had the power to do things differently and change the industry for the better.

Ultimately Tim set up a new company in competition with us and then threatened us with legal action for stopping his renewal income. The legal process was an eye opener for me. I couldn't believe that this man had completely breached all the terms of our agreement but seemed to think he had a claim against us. Unbeknown to us, during the 18 months he was working with us, he had set up the new company, transferred the income and assets of the sale and purchase agreement to it, but excluded the liabilities under it. He then dissolved the original company with whom we had signed the agreement.

I can still recall the lurch in my stomach that accompanied the arrival of each letter from his solicitor. Then the debilitating mixture of anger, frustration and disbelief that distracted me from the important task of running the business but was seemingly impossible to quash. Looking back now, I shudder at the thought of the whole sorry episode. It cost me tens of thousands of pounds and made me question my confidence in people, society and the legal system, but it also taught me a very important lesson.

CHAPTER 4

What's It All About?

Questions

I have always been a dog person. Back in 2003, after I had ditched the M25 commute, Colin and I decided we were in a position to take on a puppy.

Alfie spoilt us. He never went to the loo in the house as a puppy, despite us not formally house training him. He didn't cry at night and he was quite content to be left on his own for a few hours if we needed to go out. He was very loyal and loving and his sole purpose in life was to please us.

In August 2013, after jumping and weaving at his agility class as well as he always had, he wasn't quite himself on the Saturday morning. I booked him a slot with the vet in no way prepared for what was to come. He had Hemangiosarcoma – cancer of the blood vessels that had invaded his liver, kidneys and spleen. The vet had immediately recognised a ruptured spleen, but had hoped to resolve it by operating on Alfie. When he opened him up he realised why he was bleeding, and the extent to which the cancer had spread. He called me, with Alfie still on the operating table, and told me that the kindest thing to do was not to wake him up.

Looking back, if that was his time to go then he went in the best way he possibly could have. Although the shock was hard for us to deal with, it would have been much harder on him to suffer a prolonged period of illness. He was so tuned into our emotions that he would have known exactly what was happening with one look into my eyes.

The shock of the sudden loss of a family member was a raw experience. It was completely unexpected and knocked me for six. This, along with the frustration of Tim dominating my thoughts, prompted me to question what was really important in life. Did I want to be expending so much time and energy running a company that was barely turning a profit after taking Neil's salary, office rent, professional indemnity insurance, regulatory fees and all the other expenses into account? I wished I could spend more quality time with my children, then aged three and six.

During this period of re-evaluation, I started to do more reading. I can't remember how I came across Audible, but I am glad I did. I now listen to audio books while I am driving, out running, walking the dogs, cooking or gardening. They have provided me with insights into worlds I never knew existed, sparked ideas, emotions and ambitions in me, and ultimately encouraged me to write this book.

While I was reeling from Alfie's death and questioning what life was all about, I listened to a book called *Happiness: A Guide to Developing Life's Most Important Skill* by Matthieu Ricard. It introduced me to the concept of mindfulness and meditation.

Mindfulness

I have always been interested in psychology and the power of the mind, but never studied it past A Level. My take on Ricard's book is that happiness isn't about accruing material possessions or wealth, or even about finding a vocation you truly love; it is more about training your brain to be present in every moment.

This training is enhanced by a practice called meditation. I was aware of the existence of meditation but I had never really given it much credence. The book made me stop and take notice, even buy into the concept and want to learn more, but it wasn't until nearly a year later that I actually found myself meditating.. I was a delegate at a workshop during which I unexpectedly found myself participating in a guided meditation. I was sceptical and worried about doing it wrong or falling asleep, but after the exercise, which passed without incident, I experienced a feeling of awareness that I was interested in exploring further. I started to believe that I was capable of more and saw a way out of the stress and turmoil that was casting a shadow over my working life.

Neil and I had got to a point where Mr Timothy Green and his solicitor realised he had no claim against us. The whole sorry episode caused me a significant amount of stress as well as costing tens of thousands in cash. However, the experience itself taught me that I shouldn't feel inferior to those with apparent success. I have worthwhile methods, practices and values and I should believe in myself.

I tested this theory by signing up for a marathon.

I have always been a keen sportsperson. Athletics was my favourite sport at school, but I was a sprinter rather than a distance runner. I lost my way in my teens, but started running again while I was at university. When I moved out of halls, I kept up with the running and completed the Great North run a few times as well as a local sprint triathlon. A marathon, though, was something I couldn't quite comprehend.

When planning what marathon to enter I should probably have paid slightly more attention to the route elevation, but I made it round the Bournemouth Marathon in 4 hours, 30 minutes and 21 seconds despite the steeper than anticipated hill sections. My target was to complete the course without walking, and my words were 'I am never, ever doing that again' as my husband and children greeted me on the finishing line, but I had done it. Completing the marathon rekindled the belief instilled in me from my childhood that anything is possible.

Themes

Reflecting on my first 15 years or so in the 'grown up' world, I'm fitting the pieces of the puzzle together.

I wanted a career that enabled me to be 'me' rather than keep up appearances to impress others. I wanted to make a real difference in other people's lives and use the analytical part of my brain.

Over the years, I have had the pleasure of working with many different people at different stages of their lives. Initially my focus was on providing advice around mortgages and property finance. There is something exciting about property. I enjoy the thought of a house becoming a home, as well as the challenge of renovating and adding value. After Tristan Till had taken the shine off my property ownership journey, I wanted to make sure others found the experience more fulfilling.

Over time, the needs of my clients developed and I found myself working on a broader range of financial planning requirements, from those of young adults to retirees, and young families to widows and divorcees.

Working with individuals and couples approaching retirement was particularly enjoyable – the challenge of piecing together fifty or sixty years' worth of financial history, often in the form of numerous disparate pension pots, savings and investment plans, and bringing them together to formulate a clear financial future appealed to me. The more work I did in this area, the more interested I became and the more referrals I attracted.

Helping clients to translate dreams into reality became addictive. I could see a real need for trusted advice for those approaching retirement, particularly given the perfect storm brewing at that stage in their lives.

CHAPTER 5

The Financial Lifecycle

A typical financial journey

Before I define exactly what I mean by retirement, it is helpful to consider a typical financial journey through life.

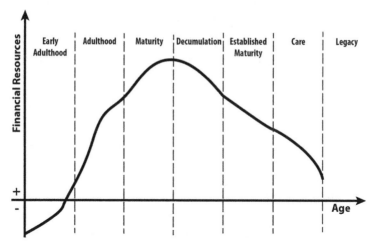

Figure 5.1 - A typical financial journey

As we start out on our own, our financial resources are usually limited and we set to work to accumulate things of value, or 'assets', to fund our future. Assets can come in many forms like cash, stocks and shares, and property (I describe the different types of asset in more detail in Chapter 7). Often early adulthood sees us struggling to pay off debts at the same time as trying to fund our future.

Once we have established ourselves financially, we tend to have to tap into some of our liquid (accessible) assets to fund the purchase of other assets, like a house to live in or a car to drive. This might mean taking on more debt. We may also find our expenditure increases at this time, for example if we start a family. Hopefully, our earning capacity is increasing too, which helps to fund the cost of living, and we might be thinking a little more about putting money aside for the future in investment vehicles such as pensions.

Later in adulthood, our finances become better established. Perhaps children have become less financially dependent, perhaps our debts have been repaid, and there is more in the way of disposable income to enjoy. We concentrate more on setting money aside for the future and pay more attention to any financial plans and policies we have put in place over time.

Historically, at around the age of 60, we make a transition out of the workforce into retirement, where we begin drawing on the assets we have accumulated to support us in the form of income or capital.

Fifty years ago, we spent a fairly short time in this decumulation phase. Our assets would typically need to support a fairly quiet retirement for five or so years before we died. These days we need our assets to support us for much longer. This might be the time in our lives that we decide to do some of the things we have dreamed of but haven't had time to do while working, like a grand design or round the world cruise. It is also becoming increasingly common for people to spend time in the decumulation phase working part-time or for part of the year.

As we age and become less physically able, our expenditure levels may reduce to support a quieter phase of life. At this time we may choose to downsize and access equity from property.

I plan to flourish in the maturity phase in good health, until one morning, when I have done all I need to do in the world, I don't wake up. The reality, however, is that health deteriorates with age, and for many, extra care and support are needed. The cost of care can be significant and a drain on our remaining assets.

Our financial lifecycle doesn't necessarily cease with our time on the earth. We may wish for our remaining assets to be passed on to loved ones after our death.

Everyone will place a different level of importance on leaving a financial legacy. To some it is worth going without during their lifetime to maximise the pot left behind, while others will see success as passing away with nothing left in the bank, having enjoyed the fruits of their labour during their lifetime.

What is retirement anyway?

The *Oxford English Dictionary* defines retirement as 'The action or fact of leaving one's job and ceasing to work', but we tend to use the term retirement in a much broader context.

Take the circumstances of these clients, who all benefitted from Find Peace of Mind's retirement planning service last year.

Debbie had a successful career in finance but gave up work 10 years ago to care for her elderly mother. With household income needs met by her husband's salary, Debbie approached me for advice about accessing a lump sum from her pension to provide a deposit on a holiday home in Cornwall.

Adrian was desperate to stop working, but didn't expect to be able to for many years. He had a number of small pension pots with ex-employers and needed advice on what they would mean in terms of a retirement income.

Terry enjoyed his job but wanted to reduce his hours to spend more time with his newborn twin grandsons. He wanted to draw a lump sum from his pensions and repay his mortgage to reduce outgoings. This would enable him to work part-time.

Sandra never believed in pensions. She built up a property portfolio during her time in employment and wanted our advice on how she could structure things to stop work and live comfortably off the rental income.

To some, retirement means giving up work; to others it means drawing on pensions. It could mean both, or something else entirely. The traditional concept of retirement is outdated and I think we need a new term to describe it, but for now, I will use the term retirement when I really mean the transition in mindset from accumulating to decumulating.

Pension arrangements

While retirement does not necessarily mean drawing a pension, one important element of retirement planning for many is their pension provision.

If you choose to contribute to a pension, or a third party such as an employer contributes on your behalf, you are accumulating value in that pension. Pensions are a tax efficient way of saving during the accumulation phase because contributions receive tax relief, but there are restrictions on when you can draw on them.

When you draw on your pension to provide an income or a lump sum, the fund is referred to as having been crystallised and it moves from the accumulation to the decumulation phase. Under current legislation it is not generally possible to crystallise a pension before the age of 55, and it is likely that this minimum pension age will be increased in the future.

Historically an individual would pay into a pension, typically provided by their employer, and when they reached retirement age they would receive a regular guaranteed income for the rest of their life.

Over the years, we have been given more and more choices over how we can access our pensions. We can have numerous pensions, some crystallised, some uncrystallised, and it is also possible to have one pension policy that includes both crystallised and uncrystallised funds. The options differ depending on whether a pension is a defined benefit (final salary) or a defined contribution (money purchase) arrangement, so it is useful to explain the difference between the two.

Defined benefit pension schemes

A defined benefit pension provides an income which is linked to the member's salary when they were in employment. For example, Sarah has worked for her employer for 30 years and was a member of her employer's defined benefit pension scheme during that time. The pension is a 60ths scheme, which means that for each of the 30 years she has been a member, she has earned 1/60th of her final salary as a pension.

When she retires after 30 years' service, Sarah's salary is £50,000. She is therefore entitled to a pension of £25,000 each year (30/60 x £50,000).

Typically, a defined benefit pension will be increased each year in line with inflation and will provide a dependent's pension to a spouse if the member dies. As the population lives longer, the cost of providing a guaranteed income for life has significantly increased. As a result, many defined benefit schemes are closed to new members.

A defined benefit pension is drawn from an overall fund, managed and administered by the scheme trustees. If the stock market crashes just before she retires, Sarah's income from her pension won't be affected. It is the trustees who bear the risk and are responsible for making sure there is enough money in the pot to meet their obligations to all members as they fall due.

Defined contribution pension schemes

A defined contribution pension (also known as a money purchase pension) is more flexible than a defined benefit arrangement, but less certain. Contributions are invested in the member's choice of underlying investment funds. Each individual has their own fund which is ultimately used to buy retirement benefits.

Like Sarah, Simon has worked for 30 years, and both he and his employer have been contributing to his employer's defined contribution pension.

Simon has his own individual pension 'pot' which has a lump sum value that has fluctuated over time. When he reaches retirement, Simon can choose how he wants to draw benefits from the pension. He can use the whole fund to buy a guaranteed lifetime income (like Sarah's) or he can keep the fund invested and draw a regular income or lump sums from it. There are other options and combinations of options available too, but let's keep it relatively simple for now and come back to these other options later.

Although Simon has more choice over the structure of the benefits he receives, he bears all the risk. If his pension fund is invested in the stock market and markets crash the night before he draws his pension benefits, the value of his fund could reduce by thousands and the benefits he receives will also reduce.

CLIENT STORY
Jim

I was at Glastonbury Festival when I heard the shock news that Britain had voted for Brexit. As I emerged from my tent to prepare breakfast, I noticed numerous missed calls and messages from Jim, a client I had recently been working with to consolidate three pension pots into a single fixed term annuity. Jim was clearly desperate to speak to me so I called him back, explaining that I was out of the office and apologising for the noise of the festival goers in the background.

The stock market had fallen off a cliff and Jim's money was due to exit his three pensions imminently. Once transferred, there was no going back and he was distraught at the thought that his pension could be 20 or 30% lower than he had expected.

Thankfully, we had transferred Jim's pensions into low risk cash funds in preparation for his retirement so he was not adversely affected, but his experience really brought home to me how important this de-risking process is.

The cost of a guaranteed income

As the population lives longer, the cost of providing a guaranteed income for life increases. Unlike in Sarah's case where the scheme trustees are required to cover this extra cost, Simon ends up having to cover the cost himself.

Pension companies employ actuaries to work out what level of income should be provided in return for every £1,000 of a person's pension fund. They will look at things like how long a person is likely to live, which is affected by:

- ◉ Their state of health
- ◉ Whether they smoke
- ◉ How old they are already
- ◉ Where they live

and what rates of return the -pension company expects to be able to achieve by investing the capital sum, which is affected by:

- ◉ Inflation
- ◉ Interest rates
- ◉ Gilt yields (returns on government bonds).

Pension providers use their own experience as a starting point, but they will also factor in wider societal trends and expectations for future longevity.

Simon doesn't have to buy an income from the pension provider he used during the accumulation phase. He has an 'open market option', meaning that he can shop around – asking each of the pension providers what income they will offer in return for his pension fund. The income he is able to achieve will depend on the pension company's estimate of how much it will cost them to provide him with that income. Different pension companies will base their calculations on different data sets and assumptions, so the income available from each provider will be different. As well as having to accept the investment risk while his pension is invested in the markets, if he wants to purchase a guaranteed income, Simon must accept the risk of annuity rates changing.

Tax free cash

When pension benefits are crystallised, you have the option of drawing a proportion of your pension, usually 25% of the value of the fund, in tax free cash. You must decide whether or not to take the tax free cash when you crystallise the fund, and there is no going back on your decision. If you decide not to take the cash, that's it – you can't then choose to take it at a later date.

Although everybody's circumstances will be different, taxpayers are generally better off drawing the maximum tax free cash from a defined contribution pension. Let's take the example of Sid, who would like to crystallise his pension pot of £100,000. He has the option of drawing 25%, so £25,000, in tax free cash.

Sid chooses to take the maximum tax free cash and has a sum of £75,000 remaining to buy an income. He chooses a guaranteed lifetime annuity and A1 Insurance Company offers him £3,800 a year in return for his £75,000 fund. This £3,800 will be taxable as income.

Sid's tax free personal allowance is used up with other income and he is a basic rate taxpayer, so he actually receives £3,040 from A1 Insurance Company after tax of 20% has been deducted.

If Sid hadn't taken the tax free cash he would have had a larger pot with which to buy an annuity, so he would have been able to secure a higher income of £5,066 before tax and £4,053 after tax.

Sid's income is £1,013 higher if he doesn't take any tax free cash. However, going back to the scenario where Sid takes the maximum £25,000 in tax free cash, if he puts this sum into a bank account, even if it earns zero interest, he could draw £1,013 per year, the difference in the two income figures, for over 24 years before the cash in the bank runs out. In reality, Sid could also earn interest on this money, and if he was comfortable with taking some risk, it may be possible for him to achieve higher returns that would extend the life of the capital further.

For higher and additional rate taxpayers, the benefits are even greater.

Top tip –   some pensions that were set up prior to 6 April 2004 (A-Day) may entitle you to more than 25% in tax free cash so it is important to check on this before you draw benefits or transfer a pension into a different arrangement.

Think about – money held in pensions can be tax efficient on death, so if providing an inheritance is a primary concern, it may be worth considering retaining capital in a pension rather than drawing it as cash.

State pension

In the past, the majority of people relied entirely on their state pension to see them through retirement, but now I hear people almost dismiss the state pension as immaterial. In fact, when you look at the benefit it provides, it is actually a fairly valuable asset.

Before April 2016 there were two parts to the state pension: the basic state pension and a second part which has had various guises over the years, including the state second pension, S2P, SERP and the additional pension. April 2016 saw the introduction of the new single tier pension. An individual reaching state pension age in 2017 will receive an income of around £159.55 per week. This pension will increase each year with inflation or average earnings, whichever is the higher. At the time of writing, to achieve an equivalent guaranteed lifetime annuity on the open market, a 66-year-old would need a pension fund of £305,381.

In order to be eligible for the single tier pension, you need to have 35 qualifying years national insurance contributions.

It is possible that you could have been contracted out of the second part of the state pension in the past. If this is the case then a deduction could be applied to your state pension depending on the number of years you were contracted out.

It is sensible to apply for a state pension forecast ahead of your intended retirement to identify whether there are any gaps in your national insurance record. You can do this online at www.gov.uk and if gaps do exist you may have the option of topping up your contributions.

You can also choose to defer drawing your state pension if you do not need it when you reach state pension age. Whether or not this will be appropriate will depend on factors such as:

- How long you intend to work
- What other income sources you have available to you
- How long you intend to defer your pension for
- Your tax status.

CHAPTER 6

Pension Flexibility

There is little flexibility available to retirees drawing benefits from a defined benefit pension. They may have some discretion over the level of tax free cash they take, but in terms of the income, it is a case of getting what they are given. Likewise, other than the option to defer, the state pension is paid on a set basis and there is no option to alter it.

With a defined contribution pension, on the other hand, you are now able to choose from a wide range of options. Since April 2015 it has been possible to access the pot as a lump sum or a series of lump sums, as well as via an annuity or a flexi-access drawdown arrangement.

In this chapter, I will set out the main pension income options currently available to members of defined contribution pension schemes. Owners of a defined benefit pension can only achieve this flexibility if they convert it to a defined contribution arrangement. This is unlikely to be advantageous so should be considered extremely carefully. Because of the complexity of such a decision, anyone wishing to consider it is required to seek professional advice if the value of their fund exceeds £30,000.

Lifetime annuity

Traditionally pension pots were used to purchase an annuity. In return for the value of your pension fund, after the deduction of tax free cash if you have chosen to draw it, the annuity provider agrees to pay you a guaranteed level of income for the rest of your life. You can choose to include death benefits, such as spouses' pensions, or guaranteed benefits, regular increases to income to offset the impact of inflation, and how you wish the income to be paid (e.g. monthly or annually). The choices you make will affect the starting income you receive.

The benefit of an annuity is that the income will continue for the rest of your life so you do not need to worry about outliving your money. However, if you die early and you have not selected any death benefits, the full value of your pension fund is lost. Traditional annuities are inflexible and, once in place, cannot be altered.

If you are a smoker or suffer from certain medical conditions, for example high blood pressure or high cholesterol, you may qualify for an enhanced or impaired life annuity. The income available from these annuities will be higher than under a standard annuity, reflecting your reduced life expectancy.

Top tip – even if you do not believe your life expectancy to be affected by underlying medical conditions, it is worth completing a medical questionnaire if you are considering applying for an annuity because even a minor condition may mean you are able to qualify for a higher income.

CLIENT STORY
Jacquie

Jacquie is the first to admit that she is a worrier by nature. When it comes to her finances she needs to know exactly what she has, and that it is not going to fall in value.

When she began thinking about retirement, her key requirements were:

⊘ To know that she would receive an income for the rest of her life, no matter how long she lives (her mum is 99 and there is a history of longevity in the family)

⊘ To know her pension wasn't going to reduce.

Although she would like to have secured a higher income than was achievable from a lifetime annuity, she weighed up the pros and cons and decided that she wouldn't be able to sleep at night if she used her pension fund to buy anything other than a guaranteed income for life.

Flexi access drawdown

It is now possible to invest your pension funds in a drawdown arrangement and draw on them flexibly. You could, for example, draw capital from your pensions immediately but defer drawing an income, and you can adjust income as required from year to year or to support changes in your lifestyle.

Flexi access drawdown arrangements enable you to keep any funds not being drawn as cash invested for the future. This does mean, however, that those funds will be exposed to investment risk. It is possible to tailor the level of risk to suit your individual profile, but generally speaking the charges that apply to drawdown accounts require some level of risk to be adopted in order to make the investment worthwhile.

CLIENT STORY
Andrew

Andrew had built up a number of defined contribution pension funds over the years. He had taken early retirement from his role as a consultant and was receiving a regular income from a final salary pension.

Andrew's wife was still working and their household income was nearly manageable, but they had been drawing on their cash savings to supplement income and these were now depleted. The couple needed a small amount of additional income from Andrew's pensions just to give them a bit more flexibility, and they hadn't yet repaid their mortgage which was costing a significant amount each month.

Andrew was reluctant to purchase an annuity with his defined contribution pension funds, knowing that when his wife stopped work they would be in need of a higher level of income. He also wished that at least some of the value of his pensions could be passed on to his children after his death. This was of particular concern to him because he suffers from a heart condition which he is aware reduces his life expectancy.

As a medium risk investor, Andrew was happy to have his pension funds exposed to the markets and comfortable with the thought of their value fluctuating over time. He needed his funds to:

- Improve monthly cash flow

- Provide an inheritance for his children

- Provide the opportunity for investment growth and the potential for a higher level of income in the future.

After a detailed analysis of Andrew's circumstances, we put a plan in place to consolidate his pension arrangements into a single flexi-drawdown account. Andrew withdrew the maximum tax free cash from the fund which was just enough to repay the couple's mortgage and provide a cash buffer.

With the mortgage repaid, Andrew's household expenditure dropped to a level which meant income was more than sufficient to cover it without any further income from his flexi-drawdown fund. The fund is still invested and steadily increasing in value, providing the potential for income in the future as and when it is required.

Uncrystallised pension lump sums (UFPLS)

As long as pension providers are willing to facilitate it, you are able to draw lump sums from uncrystallised pension funds. Of any UFPLS, 25% is tax free and 75% is taxable as income.

You can even draw the whole value of your pension as a lump sum, but, as Bob's story demonstrates below, this can result in a hefty tax bill.

CLIENT STORY
Bob

Bob contacted me because he wanted to draw his pension, which had a fund value of £100,000, in full. I explained that if he took the whole fund as a lump sum he would receive £25,000 tax free and the other £75,000 would be taxed as income.

Bob had no other taxable income for the 2017/18 tax year so would be taxed as follows:

> £100,000 withdrawn
> £25,000 (25%) tax free cash
> £75,000 taxed as income
> £11,500 tax free
> £33,500 taxed at 20% (£6,700 in tax)
> £30,000 taxed at 40% (£12,000 in tax)
>
> Total tax bill £18,700

Of his £100,000 fund, Bob would receive £81,300 after tax.

Instead of taking the whole fund straight away, Bob decided instead to take one immediate lump sum of £50,000 and a second after the end of the tax year, realising that if the fund value remained the same, his tax bill would reduce to £10,400.

> Year 1 (£50,000 withdrawn)
> £12,500 (25%) tax free cash
> £37,500 taxable as income
> £11,500 tax free
> £26,000 taxed at 20% (£5,200 in tax)

Year 2 (£50,000 withdrawn)

£12,500 (25%) tax free cash
£37,500 taxable as income
£11,500 tax free
£26,000 taxed at 20% (£5,200 in tax)

Total tax bill £10,400

As part of our planning we put the £50,000 Bob didn't draw straight away in a low risk fund to minimise the chance of it falling in value. Investment returns were limited because of the low risk approach, but the £50,000 that stayed invested did achieve a return of £1,000, meaning that when Bob came to draw the second lump sum, the fund was worth £51,000.

On the first lump sum, Bob received £12,500 in tax free cash, but because of the investment growth, Bob's tax free cash entitlement on the second lump sum was £12,750. Had he left the fund for longer, his entitlement to tax free cash may have grown larger.

Fixed term and flexible annuities

It is possible to access tax free cash and lock into a pension product that provides some level of guarantee, either in relation to the value of the underlying fund or the level of income, or both, as well as some degree of flexibility in the level of income over time. It is also possible to opt for zero income from your pensions for a fixed period of time, with a guaranteed maturity value available at the end of the term to be used to provide income in the future.

This type of 'middle ground' product can be useful if you prefer not to take any investment risk but still wish to access cash from your pensions, as was the case for Frank.

CLIENT STORY
Frank

Frank contacted me shortly after he had retired from his position in the NHS. He was receiving his NHS pension which was sufficient to cover his regular household bills, but he and his wife found themselves unable to afford the five star holidays comfortably that they had enjoyed while they were working. In five years' time, Frank would receive his state pension which would provide the couple with an additional £8,000 each year. This would be about what they needed to fund the holidays they desired, but they didn't want to have to wait for five years before being able to enjoy them.

Frank had a defined contribution pension fund which he wanted to access to provide a holiday fund. His preference was for zero risk – he didn't want the worry of an income that was affected by investment returns, but a guaranteed lifetime annuity wouldn't provide enough income to fund their travels.

We set up a fixed term annuity providing Frank with a tax free lump sum and a guaranteed income of £10,000 a year for five years, taking him to state pension age. After five years, Frank's pension fund would be exhausted, but in the meantime he received a known regular income to fund holidays and travel.

CHAPTER 7

Core Financial Concepts

As much as I would like to avoid financial jargon completely in this book, there are some financial concepts that it is useful to understand when considering your retirement options. This section sets out the most important concepts in a straightforward and easy to understand way.

You may well already be familiar with some or all of these concepts, so feel free to skip over this section if you wish. You could also use it like a glossary to refer back to if anything in the following chapters requires further explanation.

Compound interest

If you have money saved in a bank account, the bank will pay you interest on your savings. Let's say you have £1,000 saved and the bank account pays 1% interest each year. After a year you will have earnt £10, and your savings are now worth £1,010. If you don't draw anything out of your account, during the second year you will be earning interest on the higher balance of £1,010, so in year two you earn £10.10 in interest. In year three, again assuming you don't draw anything out, the interest you earn on your savings will be £10.20. This compounding effect, earning you interest on your interest on your interest, continues.

If you invested your £1,000 for 10 years, earning 1% interest each year, it would be worth £1,104.62 at the end. Without the compounding effect, 10 years interest at 1% a year would be £100, but because you are earning interest on your interest, you earn a little more.

Inflation

When I was at school, I used to get £1 a week pocket money which was pretty generous. It enabled me to walk to the 'Tuck Shop' about a mile from my house, buy a magazine and enough penny sweets to keep me going until I got home. Now I would need at least three times as much to be able to buy the magazine, and I probably wouldn't have much change for sweets.

Inflation measures the rate at which the price of goods and services bought by households rises or falls. It is measured by the Office for National Statistics (ONS) which takes a 'shopping basket' of items that are representative of consumer spending patterns. The items included in the shopping basket are adjusted over time to make sure they are representative, and in 2016 they numbered around 700 items. The prices of these items are collected from over 140 locations around the UK as well as from online and telephone based outlets.

As the prices of the individual items in the basket change over time, the cost of the overall basket changes, and it is this change that is reflected in the inflation figures.

There are different measures of inflation which consider slightly different shopping baskets. The Consumer Prices Index (CPI) is the measure now used in the UK Government's target for inflation, and its basket excludes mortgage interest payments and housing costs. The Retail Prices Index (RPI) is the longest standing measure of UK inflation. Its basket includes mortgage interest payments.

Asset classes

An asset is something of value owned by an individual or company that can be converted into cash. In the context of our personal finances, assets tend to be categorised into four main types.

Cash. Cash itself is an asset – it has a value and can be exchanged for goods and services. Cash can be held in a bank account and will attract interest, payable to the owner.

Shares (or equities). A share in a company represents an 'ownership interest', so shareholders are part owners of the company. Take Sainsbury's as an example. Sainsbury's has 2,186,840,000 shares in issue (in existence), so if you own 100 shares in Sainsbury's, you own 0.0000045728% of the company.

Although your ownership is negligible, you will still be entitled to your share of the company profits, and these are paid out in what is known as dividends. Sainsbury's Board of Directors will decide, depending on how much profit has been made during the year as well as other complex factors, what will be paid out to shareholders as a dividend.

Dividends can be paid either annually, biannually or quarterly depending on the company. During 2015/16, Sainsbury's paid dividends of 12.1p per share – 4p was paid in December and 8.1p in July.

In order to buy shares in a company, you must pay for them, and the price you need to pay changes on a daily basis. Figure 7.1 shows the Sainsbury's share price between March 2016 and March 2017.

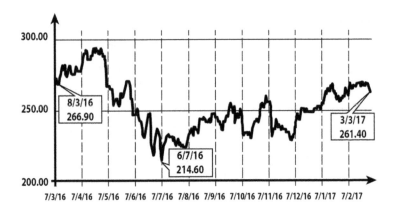

Figure 7.1 - Sainsbury's share price

If you'd bought a single Sainsbury's share on 8 March 2016 it would have cost you 266.90p. The same share would have cost you 214.60p if you had bought it on 6 July 2016 and 261.40p if you had bought it on 3 March 2017.

It is the fluctuation in the value of the share price that provides the investor with the opportunity to grow the value of their investment. If you bought a single share on 6 July 2016 for 214.60p and then sold it on 3 March 2017 for 261.40p, you would have made a return of 46.8p. If instead of a single share, you had bought 1,000 shares, you would have made 46,800p (or £468) on top of any dividends paid during the period.

There is also a risk with investing in company shares as the value of your investment can fall as well as rise. If you had bought 1,000 shares on 8 March 2016 for 266.90p each and then sold them on 6 July 2016 for 214.60p each, you would have lost 52,300p (or £523).

Because of the significant fluctuation in the value of shares, it is generally recommended that you spread your investment across a number of different shares rather than investing in a single company. Also, only invest in shares if you intend to remain invested for the medium or long term.

Fixed interest securities (also called bonds). When you buy a fixed interest security, you are effectively lending money to the government or a company. In return for the loan, the borrower will pay a fixed rate of interest for a set period of time.

Government bonds are a type of fixed interest security called gilts. In January 2017, the UK Government decided to raise £4,500 million, issuing 45 million bonds at £100 each. This particular issue of gilts is referred to as '1¾ Gilt 2057' as they will pay an interest rate (known as a coupon) of 1¾% until the maturity date in 2057.

Imagine you purchased one of these bonds. In return for your £100, which the government can now spend on running the country, you are entitled to 1¾% in interest each year (split into two payments across the year) – a whopping £1.75. If you keep hold of the bond for 40 years until it matures in 2057, you will get your £100 back.

The reality is that you are unlikely to want to keep hold of your bond for the next 40 years, so you can buy and sell gilts on what is known as the secondary market. If you decide to sell the gilt after a year, the price you can sell it for will depend on how attractive it is to buyers, which will be influenced by interest rates, inflation and general expectations in the economy. If the gilt is attractive (e.g. if it is paying a higher coupon than you are able to achieve from another gilt with a similar maturity date) then you might be able to sell it for more than the £100 you paid for it. If the gilt isn't attractive then you may have to sell it for less than you paid for it.

There are many different types of gilt available, with different maturity dates and different interest rates, that can be bought and sold on the secondary market. The coupons of some gilts are linked to inflation and these are known as index linked gilts.

Fixed interest bonds can also be issued by companies, and these are known as **corporate bonds**. In exactly the same way as the government does, the company borrows money from investors and in return pays a fixed rate of interest over a set period of time. Like gilts, corporate bonds can be bought and sold on a secondary market and there are many different bonds in issue.

Fixed interest securities are generally less risky than equities, but there are risks to be aware of when investing in them. The first is the fluctuation in the underlying value of the bond caused by changes in interest rates and inflation. As we saw above, if you pay £100 for a bond and want to sell it, you might not get back the £100 you paid for it. On the flip side, you might get more than £100, and this provides the potential for capital growth.

A second key consideration is the default risk: the ability of the borrower (e.g. the company or government) to continue making interest payments and repay the loan when the bond matures. If a company suffers financial difficulty and is unable to meet its obligations, it may default on its loan repayments and investors will lose money. Government bonds have a lower default risk than corporate bonds because countries are generally more secure than companies.

The creditworthiness of the borrower will influence the coupon paid. A company would need to pay a higher rate of interest to investors than the UK Government because of the increased risk to the investor, and a small or young company would need to pay a higher rate than an established long standing company. Bonds are allocated a credit rating to provide investors with an indication of the issuer's creditworthiness. Different credit ratings agencies use different rating scales, and Wikipedia provides this useful summary table: https://en.wikipedia.org/wiki/Bond_credit_rating

Moody's		S&P		Fitch	
Long-term	Short-term	Long-term	Short-term	Long-term	Short-term
Aaa	P-1	AAA	A-1+	AAA	F1+
Aa1		AA+		AA+	
Aa2		AA		AA	
Aa3		AA−		AA−	
A1		A+	A-1	A+	F1
A2		A		A	
A3	P-2	A−	A-2	A−	F2
Baa1		BBB+		BBB+	
Baa2	P-3	BBB	A-3	BBB	F3
Baa3		BBB−		BBB−	
Ba1		BB+		BB+	
Ba2		BB		BB	
Ba3		BB−		BB−	
B1		B+	B	B+	B
B2		B		B	
B3		B−		B−	
Caa1	Not prime	CCC+		CCC	
Caa2		CCC			
Caa3		CCC−	C		C
Ca		CC			
		C			
C		D		DDD	
/			/	DD	/
				D	

Figure 7.2 - Credit rating tiers from Wikipedia.

Bonds that are rated as BBB- or higher by Standard and Poor's, or Baaa3 by Moody's, are considered to be investment grade bonds likely to meet payment obligations. Bonds that do not achieve this rating are classed as high yield or junk bonds and have a much greater risk associated with them.

Property. Many people invest directly in property by purchasing their own home. It is also possible to invest in property to let. This may be residential property, let to an individual or a family, or commercial property let to a business or an individual conducting business at the premises.

Investment property generally attracts a regular income in the form of rent, and owners can also benefit from the increase in the value of the property itself.

CLIENT STORY
Clive

Clive bought an investment property in 2012 for £200,000. The property is let out and the tenant pays Clive £850 each month in rental income.

After five years, Clive decides to sell the property, which is now worth £250,000. He has benefitted from the rental income of £51,000 during the five years he has owned the property, and capital growth of £50,0000.

On the face of it, this is a good return – 50% over five years, but Clive has also had costs. He took out a mortgage to enable him to buy the property and this cost him £26,250 in interest over the five years. He also had to pay for maintenance to the property and cover the cost of agents' fees, in total a further £10,000. Clive was lucky because his property was always tenanted, but investment property comes with the risk that it won't attract a tenant for a period of time, which means no rental income. His property is currently on the market, and only time will tell whether he is able to sell it for the price he wants to achieve.

Another key risk with property is that it is illiquid – meaning its value can't be realised quickly. Even if Clive secures a buyer, the legal process is likely to mean the sales process will take at least two to three months before it is completed and he has the cash in his bank.

As well as investing in property directly, it is possible to achieve exposure to the property market by buying shares in property companies or real estate investment trusts (REITS), or by investing in property funds.

Diversification

Picture a little white hen, Beatrix Potter style, delivering her eggs to the good folk of her village. Having spent lots of time taking orders then laying these eggs, the little white hen wants to get them delivered as quickly as possible to her customers, so she stacks her basket high with all 10 eggs she needs to deliver and sets off down the steep slope.

Unexpectedly, she trips on a stone and releases the basket from her grip, sending the eggs crashing down the hill. When she eventually locates all the eggs, only two remain intact with the other eight smashed or cracked.

If the little white hen had decided not to put all her eggs in one basket, she would have avoided being left with only two of them. Her trip would still have cost her the majority of the eggs in one basket, but she would have had a smaller number of eggs in each basket.

The principle of diversification in investment markets is similar. If you put all your investments into a single asset class and that asset class reduces in value, then you lose a lot, whereas if you invest only some of your capital in that asset class, you lose a lesser amount.

If you invest in a number of different assets at the same time, you are spreading the risk. If one asset class falls in value, another might rise, meaning that the loss you have made in one area is offset by the gain you have made in another.

Some asset classes are highly correlated, meaning that as one rises, the other also rises. Some have a low level of correlation, so one might rise while the other shows no significant change. Some can be negatively correlated, meaning that as one rises, the other falls, and vice versa.

By carefully combining different asset types, you can reduce risk and therefore achieve superior returns.

Collective investments. As well as diversifying across a number of different asset classes, it is possible to diversify your investment within each asset class.

Let's say you want to invest in shares of UK companies (UK equities). You could invest in a single UK company, or in a number of companies. The greater the number of companies you invest in, the lower the risk of a significant fall in the value of your investment, but it is difficult to achieve a broad spread as an individual.

Collective investment funds enable you to spread your investment by pooling your money with that of other investors. By investing for a large group, rather than an individual, the fund manager has sufficient assets to spread the investment risk.

Collective investment funds can be either active or passive. An actively managed fund is run by a fund manager, usually assisted by a team of analysts who select and monitor a portfolio of assets on the investors' behalf. If the fund manager thinks a particular market, sector or company is about to fall in value, they can reduce their holdings or sell them completely.

Active managers can also buy into industries and companies they believe to be more promising, hoping to bolster returns and minimise losses for investors.

In contrast, passive funds are run by computer and simply track an index or set of stocks based on an automated trading strategy. This generally makes passive funds cheaper but investors are stuck with the fluctuations of the index they track.

There has been much debate over whether an active or a passive approach to investing is more appropriate and there is no clear answer. Different situations require different approaches.

Investment vehicles

An investment vehicle is really a financial product used by an investor with the intention of gaining positive returns. There are many different types including bank accounts, ISAs, pensions, general investment accounts and investment bonds. Pensions are covered in some detail elsewhere in this book. Although the other investment vehicles can be extremely useful tools for achieving the lifestyle we desire in retirement, a detailed analysis of each is beyond the scope of this book.

What it is important to know is that there are a variety of financial products out there, each with different tax treatments and each providing investors with access to different underlying investment funds. It is possible to invest in a fund through different investment vehicles, and it is the investment vehicle that determines the tax treatment of the investment.

CLIENT STORY
Brian and James

Brian and James invest in the A and B UK Equity Fund. Brian holds his investment in an ISA and James holds his investment in a general investment account (GIA).

Both Brian and James receive income from the fund in the form of dividends, but James's income is subject to tax while Brian's is not because it is held in an ISA. When they come to sell their investments in A and B UK Equity fund, Brian will not be subject to any tax whereas James may be subject to capital gains tax.

Platforms/wraps

One relatively recent phenomenon in the world of investing is the investment platform, or wrap. This is really just an administrative wrapper that allows you to hold investment vehicles under a single account.

Platform providers include traditional insurance and investment companies, as well as providers that are new to the market and have developed bespoke platform solutions.

A key benefit of using a platform is that you can invest with a range of fund managers but see all your investments through a single account. It is also easier to transfer monies between accounts, for example to take advantage of annual ISA allowances.

Figure 7.3 illustrates how both an ISA and a general investment account can be held through a single platform account, enabling the investor to 'feed' their ISA as a new allowance becomes available each year.

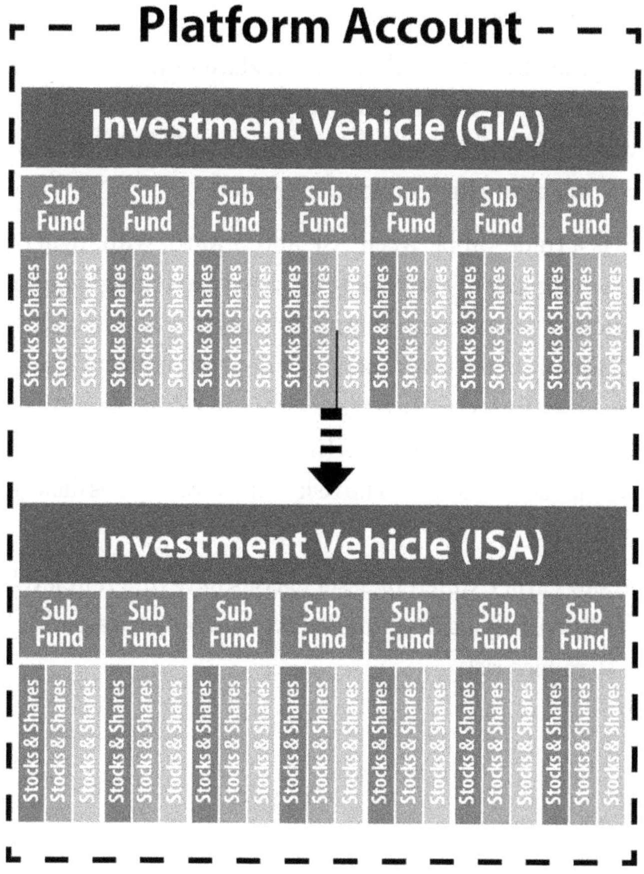

Figure 7.3 - Platform account

It is also possible to invest directly in stocks and shares on a platform as well as holding pensions and other investment vehicles.

Risk

One of the most important aspects of any investment is the level of risk it involves. We can consider risk in this context as the chance that an investment's return will be different than expected. Taking a risk means accepting the possibility that you might lose some, or even all, of your investment.

Risk is generally measured by the standard deviation of returns, so an investment providing a slow but steady return will have a low standard deviation, and an investment with wildly fluctuating returns will have a high standard deviation.

There is a trade-off between risk and reward, with higher risk approaches generally providing the potential for higher returns. Everybody feels differently about risk, and the appropriate level of risk for any given investment will depend on the tolerance of the investor (how comfortable they are in taking a risk) as well as their capacity to accept risk (how heavily impacted they will be if a risk doesn't pay off). The risk/return trade-off is illustrated in Figure 7.4.

As we saw earlier, different asset classes have different levels of risk, and diversifying investments across a range of asset classes helps to reduce risk.

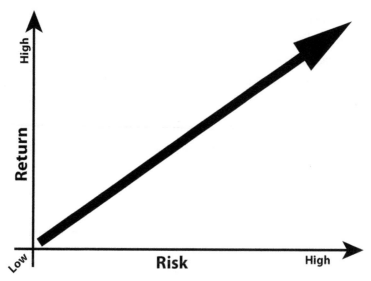

Figure 7.4 - Risk/return tradeoff

Financial strategies in later retirement

Although they may not be necessary in early retirement, it is useful to be aware of strategies that might come in handy in the future.

Equity release loans, or lifetime mortgages, are arrangements where a property owner takes out a loan secured on their property without a fixed end date to the arrangement.

The loan is repaid on the sale of the property, typically when the borrower dies or enters long-term care.

It is possible to make regular payments towards the interest costs of an equity release arrangement, but if this isn't affordable, the borrower can choose to have this interest 'rolled up' and paid from the proceeds of the eventual property sale.

We saw earlier how compound interest works – if you keep your money and interest invested, you end up earning interest on your interest. With an equity release interest 'roll up' arrangement the compounding effect is the same, but in this case it is the debt that is increasing. You are being charged interest on your interest. It is this compounding effect that can make equity release an expensive option.

Despite its cost, equity release can provide a very useful means of extracting equity from property for people who are asset rich and cash poor.

CLIENT STORY
Briony

Briony contacted me because her existing interest only mortgage was due to be repaid the following year. She had an outstanding mortgage balance of £100,000 but no savings or investments available to repay it. She was desperate not to have to move, having lived in her home for the last 50 years, but couldn't see any other option.

Now retired, Briony was surviving on her state pension and a small private pension, but had no spare cash available at the end of each month. In fact, meeting the £350 per month mortgage payments was a struggle.

After considering Briony's options and chatting with her two sons, I put in place a lifetime mortgage to repay her existing mortgage when it fell due. The ultimate value of Briony's estate will be reduced, but her sons were both in agreement that they would far rather see their mother live the life she wanted rather than give it up to protect their inheritance. Briony is now living much more comfortably with an extra £350 in her pocket each month and without the fear that she might have to move from the home she loves.

It is strongly advisable to seek professional help before entering into any equity release arrangement because the impact of doing so can be significant. Not only will such arrangements impact on the borrower's eventual estate, they can also affect entitlement to means tested benefits.

Home reversion plans are a type of equity release arrangement where a proportion of the property is sold in return for a lump sum or income. You then remain in the property as a tenant. Again this can have significant implications so it is important to take professional advice.

Long term care insurance, or a care fees plan, is a type of insurance policy that enables you to secure a guaranteed lifetime income, designed to cover the cost of care.

The cost of a plan will depend on how much income you need and the insurance company's assessment of how long you are likely to need it for. It will consider:

- The life expectancy of the life assure (which will be influenced by age and state of health)
- Current annuity rates
- The level of income required.

The income is paid directly to the care provider, and it is possible to build in increases to the income to cover future fee rises.

The key benefit of the insurance is the guarantee that, irrespective of how long the policyholder lives, a guaranteed tax free income will be paid to assist with the cost of care fees. However, in return for this guarantee, access to the capital used to purchase the annuity is lost.

The level of income provided by the insurance must be set at the outset, and if there is any change in care needs (and therefore their cost), you may be faced with a situation where the income from the insurance is insufficient.

There are a number of alternative strategies available to those who wish to fund care fees and it is important to consider all available strategies and combinations of strategies before entering into any arrangement.

CLIENT STORY
Rosemary

An existing client, Sam, approached me for help with his mother Rosemary's financial affairs. Rosemary, aged 95, had recently moved into a care home and, as her attorney, Sam was responsible for organising her financial affairs to pay for her care.

Rosemary's annual income was £10,800 and her fees at the care home totalled £46,800 per year, leaving a yearly shortfall of £36,000. Sam was covering the cost from his mother's limited savings while her house was on the market, but needed a strategy for using the proceeds of the house sale to meet the shortfall in income.

Sam's key requirements were:

- To ensure that Rosemary's care needs were met for the rest of her lifetime, without the need to make compromises in her care for funding reasons

- To make sensible decisions with Rosemary's capital so as to preserve it as far as possible.

We considered a variety of options, including:

- Investing the proceeds of the house sale and using them to provide a regular income

- Setting up an immediate long term care annuity

- Setting up a deferred long term care annuity (that would provide an income starting in the future).

After assessing all the costs, benefits and drawbacks, we put in place an immediate long term care annuity, providing a guaranteed income of £36,000 each year for the rest of Rosemary's lifetime, with a 5% increase in income each year. Provided Rosemary's care needs remained stable, and fee increases were within 5% each year, the annuity would ensure she was able to fund her care for the rest of her lifetime.

The cost of this solution left a further lump sum of £250,000 to be invested for higher returns, providing a fund which could be used to cover the cost of any additional care required in the future, or be inherited by Sam and his sister if it wasn't needed by Rosemary during her lifetime.

CHAPTER 8

The Perfect Storm

The best term I can find to describe a high level of psychological wellbeing is 'flourishing'. This encompasses the positive feelings of happiness and contentment along with the emotions of engagement and confidence. If we are flourishing, we have a sense of purpose in life; we are working towards valued goals and fulfilling our potential.

It is not about feeling good all the time since that is impossible. There will always be grief, disappointment and pain to contend with, but by achieving high levels of wellbeing, we are able to manage these negative emotions and maintain enthusiasm for life.

Level of wellbeing in society

We have experienced dramatic advances in technology and medicine over recent years, as well as general improvements in our standard of living, but our levels of happiness are not following suit.

The World Happiness Report 2016 uses sophisticated analysis to evaluate happiness, providing a score between 0 and 10, where 0 is the worst possible life and 10 is the best possible life. The UK ranked 19th of the 155 countries surveyed, with an average happiness score of 6.714 over the three years 2014–16. This was a 0.172 reduction from 2005–07.

The research reflects my experience of wellbeing among clients I meet for the first time. Although many of them are comfortable financially, they often report that they feel somewhat unfulfilled. That is not to say that they are experiencing ill-being; they are experiencing an absence of the positive rather than the existence of the negative. This is particularly prevalent in clients approaching or at retirement, a significant event in their life that forces them to re-adjust.

But what is it about our lives today that can leave us languishing rather than flourishing?

Social ideals

Never in history have we been more aware of the lives others are leading. Social media provides us with a 24/7 platform to put ourselves forward for social scrutiny and judgment, while enabling us to scrutinise and pass judgement on others.

Modern culture places huge importance on money, fame and image. Our success is generally judged against the material goods we possess, the houses we live in and the lifestyles we lead.

Social ideals are plentiful, and from a young age we are taught to aspire to them. What we see is what we believe, and there is so much to see. When I asked my six-year-old what he was going to ask Father Christmas for last year, he wanted to turn the television on so that he could answer me. He said he needed to see the adverts to know what he wanted.

Although many of society's ideals are valid and inspirational, some may not be. The ideals themselves are not the issue; it is the fact that they are inflicted upon us by society at large rather than being truly meaningful to us as individuals.

No two people are the same. Just as we each have our own unique fingerprints, we all have a unique set of values and beliefs. With our personal values there are no rights or wrongs, there are just differences.

One of my husband's highest values is football. As well as following the professionals, he is the Chairman of our local football club. He trains twice a week, plays at least one match a weekend during the season (often two), organises 120 youth players across eight teams and 100 adult players across four teams as well as coaching the under sevens team, for whom our son plays. The amount of time he spends on football related duties is significant, and we often comment on how lucky it is that he works from home most days, which provides him with the flexibility to be able to do it.

However, I'm not sure that luck really has that much to do with it – when we look closely, our lives reveal a lot about our highest values, and he has subconsciously structured his life to support him in doing the things that matter to him most.

I don't think Colin would have married me if I didn't have some interest in football, but it isn't one of my highest values. I know some so-called football widows who get thoroughly fed up with their football obsessed husbands, but there is nothing to say that Colin's love of football is any less valid than my obsession with health. Even though many of us have different values, the same activities can support them. I have taken on the mantle of admin manager for my daughter's football team and I watch my son play as much as I can. These football-related activities fit with my highest values of family and health at the same time as supporting my husband in one of his highest value activities.

My mum is a keen gardener and advocate of sustainable living. She grows her own fruit and veg and spends much of her time planning, researching, designing, planting, weeding and tending to her 6-acre plot. My dad supports her sustainable lifestyle, but holds a particular interest in the very different field of extreme sports such as kite surfing and ski kiting.

My dad manages the household finances meticulously, an activity my mum doesn't see as being strictly necessary in such minute detail. He won't bat an eyelid at spending hundreds of pounds on a new top-of-the-range kite, but might express shock at the cost of a trip to the garden centre. Each of us may have an opinion as to which person's point of view is more valid, but this would only be reflective of our own values system rather than an absolute truth.

Although if you think about it, you are likely to be able to identify some of the things you value most, it is often quite tricky to get to the bottom of what you truly value. We will explore this in more detail later.

Life in the fast lane

Perhaps one of the reasons we are not really tuned into our intrinsic values is that we rarely have the time to sleep, let alone stop and think.

We are always 'doing' something, whether it be commuting, working, shopping, DIY, cooking, cleaning or socialising. Life is run to a strictly disciplined timetable into which everything fits as long as nobody is ill or the car doesn't break down. To fit anything else in we have to reduce the amount of time we spend on important activities like sleep. The average sleep duration in the UK is 6.8 hours rather than the optimum 7.7 hours, according to the Royal Society for Public Health.

We can now access hundreds of TV channels at the touch of a button; we have news on tap 24 hours a day; we can update the world on what we ate for breakfast, lunch and dinner and send a video message to a global audience at the click of a mouse. All this technology has made life more efficient, so much more is now possible, which gives us much more to do.

In itself, our constant need to connect can be responsible for disconnecting us from what is really important. When I pick up my children from school, I am now confronted with a sign that reads 'Greet your child with a smile, not a mobile'. Absolutely true, but scary that we should even need to be told.

Longevity trends also play a part in the demands of modern life, placing responsibilities on us as carers for older friends and relatives. In 2006, the Queen wrote 192 100th birthday cards; in 2015 she wrote 9,000, as well as 1,967 105th birthday cards.

For the so called 'sandwich generation' there is a double, or even triple, whammy of responsibility. Many of my clients in their 50s and 60s find themselves still supporting their children, at the same time as caring for parents or other elderly relatives, and all while possibly still working themselves. Others find themselves replacing the 9–5 with childcare duties for grandchildren.

With our lives so fast paced and full of responsibility, it is no wonder we may have forgotten to breathe and take stock of what really matters.

Choice paralysis

In Chapter 5 we touched upon the vast range of options now available to us with our pensions, but it is not only pensions that we can use to support us in the decumulation phase. Many of us have the option of accessing income or capital from property, investments and savings.

Although choice is generally welcomed, too much choice can lead to 'choice paralysis' and reduced satisfaction with decisions, even if the decisions are good ones.

In 2000, psychologists Sheena Iyengar and Mark Lepper conducted a notable study. They set up a display of gourmet jam at a food market, offering shoppers samples and a coupon for money off any jam purchased. On one day they displayed 24 varieties of jam; on another day they displayed only six. The larger display attracted more attention than the smaller one, but those who saw the smaller display were 90% more likely to buy the jam.

This result has been confirmed by other studies and statistics. As the variety of snacks, soft drinks and beers offered at a convenience store increases, sales volumes decrease.

If we extend this psychological principle to our finances at retirement, with the increase in options available to us, the chance of us actually making a choice diminishes. Furthermore, studies have concluded that even where we do make a choice, there is a negative correlation between the number of options from which we have chosen and our levels of satisfaction with our choice.

So how can you negotiate your options at retirement to ensure you actually make choices, those choices are the right choices and you won't be dissatisfied with those right choices?

Breaking the cycle

In our fast-paced lives and fighting against the media tsunami, we need to stop and take a moment to reconnect ourselves with what is truly important to us. The run up to retirement can often be a trigger for this, providing us with an ideal opportunity to take stock as we enter a new phase of life – the shift from accumulation to decumulation.

The identification of, and connection with, our values is in itself a valuable and potentially life changing exercise. Taking this one step further and aligning our personal finances to support these values provides us with a defined path for living by them.

The process of financial planning can only be appropriate if it is done with a full and deep understanding of an individual's highest values. Likewise, genuine fulfilment and the ability to flourish in life can only be achieved if our personal finances are structured to support our highest values. I describe this movement as 'Mindful Finance'.

Mindfulness has become a bit of a buzzword of late. Although I admit to being a mindfulness convert, that's not what I am trying to get at with the concept of Mindful Finance. The word mindful is defined as being 'conscious or aware of something'. Only by being conscious and aware of our highest values and our true purpose can we structure our personal finances to deliver the life we want to lead.

Taking the wider concept of Mindful Finance with the combination of my experiences, research and insights over the past 15 years, I have developed the RETIRE process: a structured six-step process that provides a fresh perspective on planning your retirement, and ultimately a clear and inspiring foundation for enjoying life. The RETIRE process will guide you through the key components of building a fulfilling financial plan and provide you with tools and techniques to design and realise a life that is genuinely yours.

PART 2

THE RETIRE PROCESS

CHAPTER 9

The Guiding Principles

The RETIRE process sets out six clear steps to work through in planning, implementing, and realising your desired lifestyle into retirement and beyond. By taking each component in turn, understanding it in more detail and how it impacts on the wider system, you can develop an inspiring foundation for a fulfilling retirement.

The Mindful Money Tree

A key concept in the RETIRE process is the Mindful Money Tree. This concept has applications across a number of the steps and is valuable in highlighting why we should be taking a more mindful approach to personal financial planning.

The Mindful Money Tree represents an individual's relationship with their personal finances.

The tree's trunk is your true identity, your core – that intangible inner essence of your being. This unquantifiable essence can be nurtured by the fulfilment of your unique highest values.

The individual branches reflect the different aspects of your life – the means by which you can realise your highest values. Although individual values will be different for everyone, the branches through which we can connect with our values are common to us all. Upon these branches grows the fruit, in whatever form it takes for you, and the fruit is the ultimate goal – fulfilment.

Figure 9.1 - The Mindful Money Tree

A tree requires the right mix of water, nutrients and environment to thrive and produce fruit. The roots of your Mindful Money Tree absorb sustenance in the form of money and other assets, and your tree will thrive in an environment of good financial planning, but the key thing to note is that the money is not the fruit. You will require some money to grow the fruit, but a fulfilling retirement is the hoped for harvest.

The RETIRE process

I will provide a brief explanation of the different steps in the RETIRE process below, with a more detailed exploration of each step, and the tools available to assist you, in the chapters that follow. The focus of this book is on the 'reconnect' and 'evaluate' stages in the process since these elements have the greatest impact on your relationship with your finances, but are the least well documented.

Figure 9.2 - The RETIRE Methodology

Reconnect. Reconnecting yourself with your highest values is the first and most fundamental step in being able to identify the life you want to lead. If you are pursuing social ideals rather than your own highest values, you will be left unfulfilled, confused about your choices and with a lack of direction or purpose. Once you reconnect with what you truly value, daily activities become more enjoyable, choices become easier to navigate and life takes on greater meaning.

Evaluate. The evaluation stage is about developing a clear picture of where you currently stand and whether your finances are aligned to support your values.

Translate. The translate stage is about decoding the hard financial facts into meaningful personal outcomes. Once you know where you are now as well as where you want to be, you can set specific goals and actions, providing a clear strategy for achieving the retirement you desire.

Implement. Putting plans into action is the obvious next step, but it can be one of the hardest to follow through. It can be made more difficult than it should be by the complexity and jargon adopted by many financial services providers. Don't be put off. Unless you see your plans through, you will not realise your dreams.

Realise. Do not take the realise component for granted. With your strategy in place, you are free to realise the life you want to lead, but it can sometimes take work to be present in your chosen lifestyle.

Evolve. Evolution, social as well as biological, has been happening for millions of years, and it is naïve to think that retirement plans will stay the same for ever. We change, our circumstances change, our experiences, relationships and ambitions change, sometimes gradually and sometimes dramatically. Change is inevitable, so it is important to ensure your retirement plan remains on track into retirement and beyond.

The purpose of the RETIRE process is to select, cultivate and grow the fruit of your Mindful Money Tree. Now that the six steps are clear, we can delve deeper into the first component.

CHAPTER 10

Reconnect

Before we can align our personal finances with our highest values, we must first know what those values are. I have come to realise that understanding our highest values is not as straightforward as just asking ourselves what they are. Before we even start to put a label on the things that hold most importance in our lives, we must consider how our mindset can influence our perceptions, beliefs, aspirations, and our interpretation of our values.

Your tree's roots – your mindset

The connection between a tree and its food source is the root system. The roots of your Mindful Money Tree represent your mindset around money. Each of us has a different history with money, and all of our financial interactions, expectations and ambitions are filtered through this mindset. Your vision of what constitutes a happy life and what it is possible to achieve is framed by your history and perception.

If you place a swarm of fleas into a jar, they will jump, and if you don't place a lid on the jar, they will jump out. If, however, you do place a lid on the jar, the fleas will limit their jumps to stop just under the lid. If you then remove the lid, the fleas won't jump out. They have refined their behaviour to fit the restrictions of their environment, and even when the restrictions are removed, their restricted behaviour remains.

The same phenomenon is true of us humans. What we believe to be possible is a greater influencer on our achievements than our capabilities.

Take the example of running a marathon. I never believed I was capable of completing a marathon distance; it felt like an unattainable achievement only accessible to the super fit or those with serious time on their hands to train. That was until my brother took up the challenge and succeeded. The fact that someone with similar genetic make-up, personal commitments and time constraints to me could achieve it planted a seed of belief in my mind. I embarked on my marathon training still not quite convinced, but as I racked up the miles, my belief grew and grew. After completing a marathon, I realised challenges I had previously thought of as ambitious were straightforward in comparison.

In the context of your personal finances, if you believe that you will always struggle or that you need to cut back or limit your dreams in retirement, then you are limiting your possibilities. Consider the messages around money you were brought up with and what influence they might be having on your ambitions or ability to manage your money effectively.

Your tree's trunk – your identity

In order to support the fruit of fulfilment, your Retirement Tree requires a strong trunk. The trunk represents your identity.

Identity is defined as 'the fact of being who or what a person or thing is'. By its very nature, this element of your Mindful Money Tree is hard to define.

A strong sense of identity is necessary for a healthy and stable tree. Just as food is produced in the leaves on the branches of a real tree's canopy, so the branches of your Mindful Money Tree can feed and nurture your inner spirit. Your identity is strengthened by realising your highest values across a number of core aspects of being. We will explore each area of being in detail later, but first it is useful to see how living your highest vales can strengthen your identity.

In order for you to define your own highest values, I must first clearly explain what I mean by the term. The term 'values' is well-used, but often in different contexts. The *Oxford English Dictionary* defines values as 'principles or standards of behaviour; one's judgement of what is important in life'. To me, principles or standards of behaviour are very different to one's judgment of what is important in life.

If you google 'personal values', you will be presented with numerous examples, such as:

- Fun
- Ambition
- Commitment
- Cooperation
- Integrity.

It may well be that you resonate with some of these abstract terms, which are effectively social ideals. But what do they actually mean? To me maths is fun, but to many others it is not. My ambition to run a marathon just to prove to myself that I could pales into insignificance when compared with the ambition of Ben Smith, who completed 401 marathons over 401 days in 2015–16 to raise money for an anti-bullying charity.

When I refer to your highest values, I don't intend you to define them in terms of vague social ideals such as those listed above.

I refer to the specific people, things, activities or experiences that are most important to you. If you intend to work with a friend, colleague, coach or adviser to refine and implement your desired future lifestyle, then it helps if the values you define are easily understood by them, but really the key is that they are crystal clear to you.

Even by just identifying your highest values, you are more likely to live a fulfilling life because you will be more aware of and focused on them.

The Reticular Activating System

Each of us benefits from a Reticular Activating System (RAS): a complex collection of neurons at the base of our brain that tells the conscious part what specific information it should be alert to. The RAS filters all the messages entering our brain, including sounds, tastes, pictures, colours, feelings, textures – the list goes on. At any one time, there can be up to 2,000,000 pieces of information available to us, but our brains can only process so much. Our RAS picks out the pieces of information it identifies as being most important, and it sees the things we focus on as being important.

Before you read on, look around you and identify all the blue items you can see.

Have you identified all the blue items?

Now, without looking up, can you list all the green items in the room?

The green items were there all along, but your brain was working so hard on identifying the blue items that it will have filtered the green items out.

Your RAS can fuel negative beliefs, resulting in self-fulfilling prophecies. For example, if you tell yourself you can't lose weight, or that there are not enough hours in the day, your RAS will be selecting the information it needs to prove you're right. The more evidence your RAS finds, the stronger your belief becomes and the harder your RAS will be working to reinforce the belief. The compounding cycle continues and the result is that you never lose weight or have enough time.

But you can also turn your RAS to your advantage. Have you ever had a nagging question that your mind answers as if by magic? Focusing on a specific activity or goal triggers your RAS to pay attention to details that relate to that activity or goal. Simply by recognising that there are some aspects of your life that you value highly, you can set your RAS to work promoting the messages that support your highest values. But the first step is identifying what those values are.

Now that we are clear about the concept of highest values, let's get to work in identifying them.

CLIENT STORY
Julie and Ed

In the run up to their retirement, Julie and Ed were initially reluctant, even apologetic, to mention their desire to travel. Their vision of retirement was such that they felt guilty at the mention of a holiday. As part of our work together, both Julie and Ed individually identified travel as one of their highest values, so in designing their future lifestyle, we have made sure they have an adequate travel budget each year.

Now, having identified travel as one of their highest values, they often comment on how their trips, not possible while they were both working, have made life so much more fulfilling. They describe how their time spent travelling opens their eyes to new cultures, sparks their creativity and imagination, enhances their experiences when they are at home and connects them more strongly with each other.

CHAPTER 11

The Branches Of Being

In my experience working with many different people at different stages of life, I have identified six key aspects that need to be explored when searching for our highest values. These six aspects are represented by the branches of the Mindful Money Tree. Through our interactions, experiences and beliefs in relation to these aspects of being, we can grow the fruit of fulfilment. Connecting meaningfully with each of these core aspects of life strengthens our identity – the trunk of our Retirement Tree.

Vitality is about strength and energy, a life force. Physical and emotional wellbeing are key components of ensuring vitality. Without a strong life force, our attempts at fulfilment can be hampered, but with vitality on our side, our efforts can be magnified.

Attachments through meaningful connections with individuals and groups, whether it's a shared perspective, a loving relationship, an emotional connection or a competitive spark, enrich and enhance our lives.

Lifelong learning never stops. A thirst for knowledge, in whatever form is meaningful for you, is essential in achieving a sustained sense of fulfilment.

Universe and environment. The extent to which we are connected with our environment and the planet influences our overall wellbeing.

Enjoyment. Not everything has to have a serious reason behind it. I am a great believer in ensuring that sometimes we do things just for the fun of it.

Significance. We have only a finite time on earth, but our legacy can last for many years to come. Knowing that we are living a life of purpose and that we will make a lasting impression, whether socially, emotionally or financially, provides a huge opportunity for personal fulfilment.

A note of caution – a tree bearing too much fruit on any one branch may become unstable or even uprooted. For example, a loving individual who focuses so much on caring for those around her that she neglects the other branches of being puts her own health at risk.

Vitality

Vitality is a fundamental component in growing your Mindful Money Tree. The ultimate impact of poor health is death, making it impossible to live a fulfilling life in retirement in any shape or form. Our state of health not only determines whether our Mindful Money Tree can survive, it dramatically influences the tree's ability to bear fruit.

As we approach retirement, health becomes more of a concern. There is an increased risk of our bodies malfunctioning as they become older and we experience a greater number of aches and pains. With people as a society living longer, there is the need for more care in later life.

Many of us have a glass door view of what could be in store from dealing with the care requirements of our parents or other family members. This shines a light on what we might expect in later life and alerts us to the need to take care of our bodies and minds.

What we eat every day has a huge impact on our ability to flourish. There is a strong relationship between food and mood, and there is also a growing body of research linking what we eat with memory function and our chances of developing dementia. Our brains need enough fatty oils to keep them working well. They also need amino acids, found in protein, to regulate thoughts and feelings. However, it seems that new research is published every week identifying risks to our health from certain foods, and it can be difficult to navigate the expanding minefield of diets and fads. There is no one size fits all solution, but for me, a balanced diet that includes lots of fruit and vegetables while avoiding processed foods and too much sugar does the trick.

As well as being mindful of the sorts of food we are eating, it is important we consider the quality of that food. Modern farming methods are impacting on the levels of nutrition in our food. Over-farming and the use of pesticides mean that the soil has become depleted in vital nutrients. According to a 2005 report by the Independent Food Commission's *Food Magazine*, our fruit and vegetables contain an average of 20% fewer minerals than they did in the 1930s. Iron levels are down 47% in modern meat, and over 60% in milk.

Many people are deficient in certain vitamins and minerals. Because our bodies are dependent on nutrients to function properly, this can impact on our overall levels of physical and mental wellbeing. It should be possible to get the vitamins we need from our food, but it is also worth considering topping up with good quality vitamin supplements to ensure that our bodies and brains are functioning as efficiently as possible.

Like nutrition, our levels of physical activity are critical in enabling us to function effectively. Health experts report that being more active can:

- Change brain chemistry to lift mood
- Reduce your risk of stroke or heart disease by 10%
- Reduce your risk of developing Type II Diabetes by 30–40%
- Help you better regulate cortisol (stress hormone) levels
- Strengthen your internal organs, reduce cholesterol and lower blood pressure
- Strengthen your muscles and bones and reduce the risk of osteoporosis
- Improve fitness, stamina and reduce body fat
- Provide an energy boost
- Improve sleep patterns
- Reduce the risk of depression.

Not only does exercise keep our bodies fitter and less likely to malfunction, it improves our mood and cognitive abilities. It can also be a way of making social connections and having fun. The 'right' type of exercise will be different for all of us. It needs to be something we enjoy, or at least can learn to enjoy. It also needs to take into account our current physical abilities or limitations.

It is not just the traditional sports or formal exercise options that provide health benefits. Activities like gardening or walking the dog can combine physical activity with enjoyment in other aspects of your life. I am officially an exercise addict, but I haven't set foot in a gym for over 15 years. I much prefer being outdoors, connecting with the natural world and giving the dogs a run at the same time.

We can often take our mental health for granted, but our brains can benefit from a workout just as much as our bodies. One way of doing this is through the practice of mindfulness.

> '*Mindfulness is the basic human ability to be fully present, aware of where we are and what we're doing, and not overly reactive or overwhelmed by what's going on around us.*'
>
> MINDFUL.ORG

As the definition suggests, mindfulness is actually an innate ability, but it can be improved with guidance and training.

Research into the effects of mindfulness practice has historically been focused on the treatment of illnesses such as depression and anxiety, but there is also an increasing body of evidence that it can enhance wellbeing for those not suffering with mental health problems.

Mindfulness is thought to:

- Aid decision making
- Enhance productivity
- Improve strategic thinking
- Help us self-regulate thoughts, emotions and behaviours
- Improve concentration and focus
- Reduce stress and increase resilience to stress
- Improve communication skills and empathy
- Improve performance.

I described my initial scepticism about mindfulness practice in Chapter 4. Before my first experience I was intrigued, but definitely not convinced. I am now a regular user of the Headspace App which provides guided meditations to suit busy lives, and I credit it for enabling me to be a calmer, more thoughtful, more understanding and more creative person than I once was – most of the time, anyway!

We will all have very different views on what 'healthy' should look like and will place different levels of importance on the three key areas of health – nutrition, fitness and mental health. I know a retiree who competes in triathlons and another who is content to take a gentle walk around the block. They are equally happy with their levels of health.

Consider the following questions in relation to your health:

1 – What are your ambitions for your health?

- What is your ideal weight?
- How much exercise would you like to do each week?
- What type of exercise would it be?
- Are there specific challenges you would like to set yourself?

2 – What food do you choose to eat?

- Where do you shop?
- Do you buy organic produce?
- Do you avoid certain foods?
- Do you enjoy cooking?

3 – Do you practise mindfulness, or would you like to try it?

4 – Do you have any health issues? Can anything be done to improve them?

There are no right or wrong answers to any of these questions; the idea is to get you thinking about what health means to you. We can't all be triathletes, and many of us don't want to be, but how does your current state of health score against your ideal?

Attachments

The second branch on the Mindful Money Tree is all about our attachments to others, from family and loved ones to colleagues and competitors. Our relationships with others have a huge impact on our daily lives and our sense of fulfilment.

Often as we approach retirement, the dynamics of our relationships are changing. Our children may now be completely independent, and after we've supported them for much of our adult lives, there is perhaps a transition towards them supporting us. Our past role as a child being supported by our parents is a fading memory as our parents may require more support from us. These role changes can be hard to adjust to, but are a natural part of life.

- ⊘ List the ten most important people in your life. Include specifics – I want names!

- ⊘ How do you connect with them?

- ⊘ What is your relationship to each of those people and how might it change?

- ⊘ What do you want to give to that relationship?

- ⊘ What do you want to receive in return?

As well as those closest to us, there are often other people in our lives who play an important role in enabling us to lead a fulfilling life.

I recently embarked on a mentoring course through which I was required to work with a group of likeminded entrepreneurs. Having been self-employed for almost all of my working life, based from home and a definite introvert, surrounding myself only with my closest friends and a few well-known colleagues, I was initially very uncomfortable at being forced to share my aims, opinions and beliefs with a bunch of strangers.

I am so happy that I did. Without the challenge of the environment, I would never have written this book for a start. Sometimes you need to push yourself outside your comfort zone to get the most out of your relationships with others.

What social groups do you belong to? Are there community groups that are important to you? Which individuals or groups could challenge you in a positive way?

Although relationships with others can provide a positive support, the people we surround ourselves with can also negatively affect our ability to lead a fulfilling life. According to authors like Tim Ferriss, we are the average of the five people we spend most time with. The law of averages states that the result of any given situation will be the average of all outcomes, and he argues that this is true of us as human beings. We interact with many people, but the few who are closest to us will have the biggest influence on our way of thinking and decisions.

If you surround yourself with positive people, their positivity will rub off, but if your friends are constantly negative or have no aspirations, this will eventually have a damaging impact on your energy and confidence. Although I don't advocate selecting or firing friends based on whether or not they fit your model of who you want to be, it is useful to bear this concept in mind when considering whom you spend your time with. Just being aware of the influence others can be having on your outlook and aspirations is beneficial.

One of the most important roles others can play in assisting you to lead a fulfilling life is by making you accountable. Research confirms that if you personally commit to doing something, you are 65% more likely to achieve it. If you have a specific accountability appointment with the person you have committed to, the probability of completion rises to 95%.

I challenge you, if you haven't already, to tell a friend or family member that you are reading this book, taking charge of your future and connecting with your values so that you can design and live a fulfilling life. When we reach the section on setting specific goals, make sure you communicate these goals to others, too.

Lifelong learning

In our childhood, we are constantly learning new things. We are exposed to new experiences, meet new people, learn about new concepts and take on new challenges. All of this learning sparks connections in our brain that develop us as individuals, enhance our capacity and provide a sense of wellbeing and excitement.

As we progress through life, the opportunity for new learning is reduced. We reach a point where we might feel comfortable in what we know and we stop searching for new information. We might even believe that we are too old or it is too late to try something new. For years, people have assumed that as we age, our cognitive capacity diminishes significantly, but recent research suggests that this is not the case. For people with normal brain matter, cognitive decline has the potential to be quite modest. Even for those with abnormal brain function who end up suffering with dementia, the decline in cognitive function can be significantly reduced.

Studies report a decrease in brain function when people retire. However, far from this being a natural consequence of age, researchers believe that this is because when we retire, we stop challenging our brains at a high enough level or on a frequent enough basis. Scientific evidence is emerging that suggests keeping our brain challenged through lifelong learning, for example by undertaking voluntary work or participating in exercise or other stimulating activities that instil a sense of purpose, can reduce cognitive decline.

Learning can come in many forms. We are lucky enough to live in an age where we can access information about pretty much anything at any time of our choosing, and at low or no cost. From art and photography to knitting and paper craft, psychology and meditation to nutrition and exercise, and complex technology to ground-breaking neuroscience, the possibilities are endless.

As well as educating ourselves by reading, listening to or accessing information from external sources, we can develop our skills by participating in physical, mental, musical or practical activities. Learning a new skill might be more tricky once we have passed the critical learning period in childhood, but it does wonders for the connections in our brains and stimulates positive emotional responses.

What skills or activities did you enjoy as a child? Did you play a musical instrument that you would like to pick up again, or did you always wish you could have played?

CLIENT STORY
Dad

For his 55th birthday present, my brother and I treated our dad to a kite surfing lesson. Dad had been surfing a few times in the past and had participated in other extreme sports like skiing and rock climbing, but kite surfing was a new challenge.

This taste of kiting sparked an interest which Dad has pursued over the years, and earlier this year, now almost 63, he travelled to Norway to take part in the Red Bull Ragnarok. The Ragnarok is an endurance snow-kite race. Its name is taken from an epic battle depicted in Norse mythology where only the heroes of the battlefield survived, just as only the toughest of riders will complete the required five laps of the gruelling 15km course using a kite and skis or a snowboard.

Dad was probably the oldest rider in the race, but he was the 4th placed Brit and 121st of 187 participants, many of whom had to drop out with broken kites, limbs and other ailments.

I know participating in snow-kiting endurance races won't be everyone's idea of fulfilment, but what a fantastic example of taking on a new challenge in retirement.

Universe and environment

The term 'the universe' seems all encompassing, and I suppose it is. I use the term to describe something bigger than we can rationalise; a connection with something more than humankind.

There are many aspects of the universe that fascinate me. I live on the outskirts of a rural village and we benefit from a lack of light pollution. As I let the dogs out last thing at night, I often marvel at the mesmerising display of constellations, a gleaming and shimmering reminder that we are such a small part of a much bigger universe.

Even on the earth, the wonders of nature are abundant. The complex eco-systems that sustain our habitats, the beauty all around us. If I stop and think about how we got here, how many millions of years have passed, how many genetic mutations have taken place, it blows my mind.

Connecting with the outdoors is important for wellbeing. According to proponents of environmental psychology, spending time in nature reduces stress, improving mood and cognitive performance. A study found that those who are connected to nature tend to experience more positive emotions, vitality, and life satisfaction compared to those less connected to nature.

There are so many ways of connecting with nature through travel, birdwatching, wildlife, gardening, walking, photography – whatever it might be will be food for your spirit. I am a keen runner and there is nothing I love more than an early run across the Somerset Levels, watching the sun rising from behind the bristling hedgerows and the warm breath of the cows gently rising from their nostrils in the fields as I pass. Sometimes I have to hurdle the dank, deep puddles, hoping that my landing spot will be firm grass rather than squelchy surrounding bog. Other days, I spot a rainbow. Sometimes I see rare sights such as kingfishers and once an otter. If you look, there's always something.

What aspects of your life connect you with the universe? Could you be doing more to connect with nature?

In my quest to live a more healthy and connected lifestyle, I would like to grow my own food. I have experimented with growing potatoes, tomatoes and a few herbs in the past, but never with any real planning or dedication. In these times of economic, political and social change, anything we can do to become more self-sufficient seems sensible. If it can enhance our wellbeing in the process, then all the better.

Enjoyment

Not everything has to be about rigid adherence to health, growth and development. A big part of life should be about enjoying it.

Some activities are worth doing just for the fun of them. One of my favourite fun activities is snowboarding. Living in the UK, I don't get to do it as often as I would like, but our annual ski trip is always one of the first events in the diary each year. I am never going to be an Olympic snowboarder, and even though I am now reasonably proficient, I don't go enough to improve my technique significantly, so I couldn't consider it to be a learning or development activity. I go for the fun of it – the pure enjoyment and exhilaration.

In fact, I'm sure activities that we may consider to be in the area of recreation and relaxation have wide ranging benefits across the other key areas of being. For example, our annual ski tip is a time for the family to be together, share experiences and laugh at each other's miscalculations on the slopes. It is also good exercise, so supports two of my highest values: family and health. However, that isn't why I do it.

Travel and holidays are great opportunities to relax and take part in things you might otherwise not be able to fit into your schedule, but regular relaxation is an important part of your routine. For some, relaxation may come in the form of chilling out in front of the TV, sharing a drink with a friend, a spa treatment or reading a good book.

Research published in *Canadian Medical Association Journal* found that people who enjoy life live longer. They are also at a lower risk of developing problems with activities of daily living or showing declines in physical function. It appears that enjoyment of life contributes to a healthier and more active old age.

What do you do for fun or enjoyment on a regular basis? What would you like to do? What are the less frequent events you look forward to?

Significance

Our time on this planet is short. If you consider that the earth is over 4.5 billion years old, the average lifespan of a human, being 79 years, represents 0.00000176% of that time. Time is precious, so we need to make the most of it.

The fruit of our Retirement Tree can bring fulfilment not just to our own lives, but to the lives of others. The ways in which this can be achieved are limitless. It can be done by inspiring, educating, supporting, or simply loving others, but I believe we each have a part to play in making the world a better place.

Consider the legacy of a primary school teacher. My children, aged six and nine, attend a primary school of around 120 children. I entrust them to the care of a small team of teachers who have a huge impact on not only the quality of their education, but their confidence in life and learning, their values, their manners and their behaviour.

My six-year-old son Freddie is sometimes hard to motivate when it comes to school work, but his topic over the last few weeks has been the *Titanic*. His teacher has thoroughly engaged the children in the history of the ship, giving them all a role as a passenger and re-enacting some of the events of the fateful journey. This sparked great discussions between Freddie and his classmates about which social class they belong to. Freddie was allocated the role of a first class passenger and was initially very happy to be one of the lucky ones who climbed aboard a lifeboat. That was until he realised that he had to leave some of his friends behind, even though there was space on the lifeboat, just because they were in second or third class. Yesterday, Freddie thoughtfully recounted the story of the engine workers who worked tirelessly to fuel the ship's engines with coal, despite poor conditions and impending death.

This goes way beyond teaching children facts and figures for them to recall and has a huge impact on how they develop as human beings. We are very lucky to have such engaging, passionate and caring teachers who have a positive impact on the lives of our children. I know it might not be the same for everyone.

During our working lives, the impact we have on others might be fairly clear, but as we make the transition towards retirement, we may need to adjust or re-evaluate our purpose. How will we continue to ignite the spark that is fuelled by the feeling that we are having an impact?

CLIENT STORY
Bella

As well as bringing up her three sons, Bella had been a successful teacher at a number of schools during her working life. She became a head teacher, a position at which she excelled, before taking early retirement from the profession ten years ago.

On a recent day trip to the coast with a friend, she was approached by a lady who recognised that Bella had been her child's class teacher many years previously. The lady felt that she had to speak to Bella to thank her for everything she had done for her child.

As she recounted the story to me, Bella was touched that the lady had remembered her after over twenty years, let alone recognised her and felt strongly enough to approach her. She said it was a lovely moment, but the realisation of the impact she had previously had through her work was tinged with a slight sadness that she was not able to touch people in the same way anymore.

In fact, Bella is now a fantastic educational and developmental coach, and I can personally vouch for the fact that she continues to have a huge positive impact on the lives of others through her professional work. She is also an unwavering support to her family and a trusted friend to many, and her legacy will be extensive and long lasting.

My personal purpose is to harness my expertise to inspire and empower my family, colleagues and clients to lead purposeful and fulfilling lives. I get a buzz out of playing even a small part in inspiring a passion in other people. In my working life I am lucky enough to be able to work closely with people on a daily basis to help them see their finances in a different way. Sometimes I am able to transform someone's negative relationship with finance into a much more positive one, even if it's just by balancing the books, saving them a few pounds a month, or simply providing clarity – every little helps.

What would you like your legacy to be? Who have you influenced during your lifetime? Are there ways in which you can harness your values and interests, experienced through the other branches of being, to have a greater impact on generations to come?

The six branches of being give us a basis from which to evaluate our levels of wellbeing, as well as a starting point for considering untapped opportunities for getting more out of life. To assist you in further refining your thinking and assessing your progress, I have created the Mindful Money Tree self-assessment which you can access at www.retirement-compass.co.uk.

CHAPTER 12

Structuring The Branches

Having carried out the exercises on the preceding pages, you may well have started to consider what your highest values are. Some will be obvious, but you may be struggling to refine them or make them specific enough to help you to guide your behaviour. I have spent many hours thinking about what matters to me the most, and it wasn't immediately clear.

Sometimes it is almost too obvious. You can be so ingrained in your daily activities that you take them for granted, and a methodical approach is useful in getting to the bottom of what you really value most.

The best place to start is with the life you already live which probably gives you many of the clues you need. What do you currently spend your money on? Take your last 3–12 months' bank statements and identify where you are spending your money. Many banks now enable you to download your transactions in a spreadsheet format which makes this task much easier and quicker to complete.

I would suggest starting by grouping individual expenditure items into categories, for example household bills, food, sports, hobbies (list by specific hobby), children, education, and so on. Once you have done this, colour each expenditure category by the personal value you feel it is in line with and identify the percentage of your money being spent on supporting each personal value. This exercise will also prove useful when we come on to budgeting.

You can download a free expenditure analysis template at www.retirement-compass.co.uk.

What you already spend your money on will give you a fair idea of what you value most. Ask yourself why you spend what you do and how you feel about it.

When I did this exercise, I realised that I spent far more than I had expected on food. I prefer to buy organic produce, and I will pay more to know that my food is free of chemicals and that the animals I eat have not been fed on hormones. Although I was initially shocked at the amount I was spending, when I considered why I was paying more, I felt comfortable with my choices.

Next, look at how you spend your time. Subconsciously you are likely to have structured your time around the things you value most. Consider your typical day – what activities do you undertake? Where do you do them and who are you with? Now map out a typical week in 30-minute time slots.

Colour each activity according to the personal value it is supporting and identify what proportion of your time is being spent serving each value.

You can download a free 'typical week' template and view an example analysis at www.retirement-compass.co.uk.

You are likely to find that some activities support more than one value. For example, when I take my daughter swimming, I take my laptop with me and catch up on work. I am supporting my value of family, promoting my value of health and working at the same time. Colour code according to the predominant value being supported, but bear in mind the other values as you refine your thoughts, and at the same time think about how one activity might be adapted to support other values.

Some activities might not be obviously supporting any particular value. Work is a good example of this. Work itself isn't a value, but the type of work you do and how you feel about it is likely to tell you a lot about your values.

Colour code any activity you are not sure about and give it a label. Consider which values that activity is supporting. Those values might not already be apparent from your typical week diary.

Think about the following:

◉ Why are you carrying out that particular activity?

◉ Do you enjoy it?

◉ What is it in particular that you enjoy?

◉ How have you adapted the activity to support other values?

My work provides me with the opportunity to have a positive impact on the lives of others. I am also able to challenge my brain, act as a positive role model for my children and contribute to my family's financial security. I choose to work mainly from home so that I can take my children to and from school most days.

Don't worry if your values aren't immediately clear. It may take a number of passes at these exercises and a lot of wider thinking to arrive at a concise list of values. Quite often a favoured activity that supports more than one value gives you the best clues.

Your typical week and expenditure analysis will give you a good baseline from which to bring everything together. Once you have undertaken these exercises, I would recommend you consider the following questions.

George Kinder's three questions

George Kinder is an American author, financial planner and mindfulness guru who introduced us to the concept of life planning.

In line with the principles set out in this book, his philosophy is that in order to create a meaningful financial plan, it is first necessary to understand your personal goals and ambitions. He has spent many years researching, devising and implementing the EVOKE process of life planning which he now teaches to financial planners across the world.

He uses, among other tried and tested tools, three questions with clients to get to the bottom of their goals and motivations, and I have found these questions extremely useful for getting people to think in a slightly different way about what is important to them.

With the permission of the Kinder Institute, I include the three questions below. I urge you to work through each question in turn, answering it in full before reading the next question.

Question 1 – I want you to imagine that you are financially secure, that you have enough money to take care of your needs, now and in the future. How would you live your life? What would you do with the money? Would you change anything? Don't hold back on your dreams. Describe a life that is complete, that is richly yours.

Question 2 – this time, you visit your doctor who tells you that you have five to ten years left to live. The good part is that you won't ever feel ill. The bad news is that you will have no notice of the moment of your death. What will you do in the time you have remaining? Will you change your life and how will you do it? (Note that this question does not assume unlimited funds.)

Question 3 – your doctor shocks you with the news that you only have one day left to live. Notice what feelings arise as you confront your mortality. Ask yourself, 'What dreams will be left unfulfilled? What do I wish I had finished or had been? What do I wish I had done? What did I miss?'

It is interesting how changing our perspective on the time we have left in this world really focuses our thinking. If we have deep goals or desires, they are usually uncovered in the third of Kinder's questions.

Having considered the six branches of being and worked through the exercises detailed in this chapter, you should be in a position to list what you think are your top three to five values. Here are my highest values along with their definitions:

- **Family** – I support and nurture my family, doing all I can to build avenues for them to achieve their best and lead fulfilling lives

- **Health** – I treat my body, mind and spirit with respect so that I can serve my purpose as effectively as possible for as long as possible

- **Inspiration** – I believe that each and every one of us can achieve great things and I encourage others to identify and achieve their full potential

- **Environment** – I take pride in the environment I live in and positive action to enhance and improve it, carefully considering the impact of my actions and activities on the planet.

Once you have listed your top three to five personal values, define each value as clearly as you can. Describe them as if you are already living them, even if some aspects are still aspirational.

Identify specific behaviours

You wouldn't expect a successful business to have vague goals like generate more revenue or hire more staff. It would talk in specifics, for example increase revenue by 10%, or hire two new sales people. It is the same with personal goals. A useful way of thinking about this is to give everything a number.

My clients who identified one of their highest values as travel decided that a goal would be to visit at least two new countries and spend 30 days out of the UK every year.

Where a goal is not strictly financial, it should still be specific and measurable. An example of a specific health goal might be to achieve 10,000 steps a day at least six days a week to achieve a body fat percentage below 20%, or to get eight hours' sleep a night.

Many of your 'numbers' will be relevant to your expenditure planning, which we will come on to in a later chapter. While you might not be directly accounting for non-financial goals in your expenditure planning, give consideration to all these goals to ensure that they are achievable within the financial framework you are setting.

Taking my value of family as an example, I have set the following specific goals:

- ◎ To take my children to and from school at least four days a week
- ◎ To eat dinner with my children every day we are in the house together

- To dedicate 10 minutes' individual time to each child to help them with music practice every weekday
- To read to my children at least three nights a week
- To get together with my parents at least once a week.

CHAPTER 13

Feeding Your Retirement Tree

Your financial bucket

Where does the money fit in? Often financial security is identified as a key critical aspect of our being, but it is intentionally omitted from the branches of the Mindful Money Tree.

I am not naïve enough to think that money isn't an important part of life, that it doesn't matter. It clearly does, but only to the extent that it enables you to live in accordance with your highest values.

Research carried out into levels of happiness identified that the amount of money we make does make us happier up to a point, but beyond a certain level, money does not increase levels of happiness. It is not the money itself that is making us happy. We need a certain amount to provide us with security – the more we have, the better able we are to support our highest values, but once we have enough then accumulating more does not make us happier.

Your Mindful Money Tree requires the right mix of water and nutrients to sustain it and produce fruit, and this comes in the form of your financial resources. So if you set a goal of owning a holiday home in Cornwall, you will require some financial resources to enable you to achieve your goal. Your Retirement

Tree will absorb the nutrients it requires in order to grow the fruit of fulfilment.

Paul Armson neatly sets out the concept of the bucket.

Picture a bucket containing liquid. This represents your liquid cash – it is money that is available to you to spend on the things you want or need, like rent or mortgage payments, food, clothes or holidays. It is accessible to you to draw out of a cash machine instantly, or within a week or so of making a call to your bank. The liquid sits inside your bucket in the form of bank accounts, current accounts and savings accounts, perhaps cash ISAs or investments that can be sold quickly and easily.

Over time your bucket is topped up with inflows from various sources. If you are employed, each month you will receive an inflow in the form of your salary. If you are receiving a regular pension income, that income will top up the bucket. Perhaps you own an investment property and receive income in the form of rent. It could be that you receive an inheritance or another one-off windfall.

It is important to identify what is not in the bucket. Your house for example is not in the bucket because you can't access the value in it quickly. It may be that at some point you intend to downsize and release a lump sum of equity, in which case the lump sum would then enter the bucket, but the house itself remains outside.

Your pension fund is not in the bucket while it is in the accumulation phase. When you chose to crystallise benefits from the pension, you might release part of the fund (usually 25%) as tax free cash and this can enter the bucket. Any income you then generate from the pension will top up your bucket in retirement. It is possible to convert your pension fund into a drawdown arrangement at retirement which can be used to top up your bucket more flexibly.

Any business interests also fall outside your bucket. You may be able to draw a salary of dividends from your business if you have one, but the value of the business itself cannot be easily realised so sits outside the bucket.

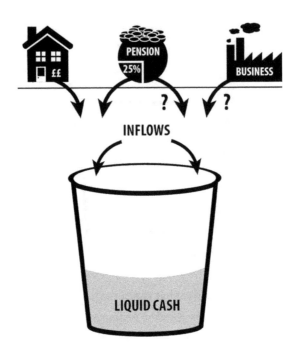

One important element of the bucket is its taps. We need to use the liquid in our bucket to cover our regular expenditure, so gradually liquid is flowing out of the tap. As well as regular expenditure, we will incur one-off costs, perhaps a new car, a child's wedding or a trip of a lifetime.

Over time the speed at which liquid flows out of the tap changes, particularly as we enter retirement. Then we may want to do some of the things we didn't get time to do while we were working, so the rate at which water is flowing out of the bucket increases.

In later life a concern for people is the cost of long term care. If health deteriorates and care is required, this can dramatically increase the flow of liquid out of the bucket.

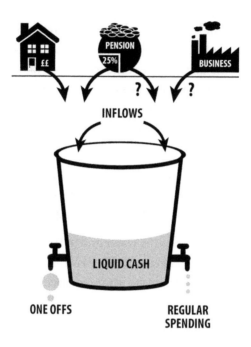

There are two key concerns in relation to the liquid level in your bucket. The most obvious is the risk that the liquid might run out. If the level at which the bucket is being topped up can't keep pace with the rate at which liquid is flowing out of the tap, the liquid runs out and we're unable to meet our expenditure needs. This situation clearly needs to be avoided.

The other important concern is that we end up with too much in our bucket. The big issue with having too much is that it means we haven't lived as fulfilling a life as we could have. Even if our sole aim in life is to provide capital to loved ones, gifting it while we are still alive and witnessing our loved ones benefitting from it would be more fulfilling than waiting until after our death to pass it on. There is also the consideration that we will end up paying tax on the liquid that remains on our death.

The concept of the bucket is used to demonstrate what the role of a good financial planner should be. It is about monitoring the level of the bucket, managing it over time so that you know how much you have got, and that it will be enough to support you in living the life you want to lead. It is as important to make sure that you are spending enough as it is to ensure you are not spending too much.

The bucket has been around for a number of years and part of its cleverness is its simplicity. However, to get the best value from it, we need to consider it in the context of the Mindful Money Tree.

The liquid in the bucket is the water and nutrients your Mindful Money Tree needs to survive and flourish. If the flow of water and nutrients isn't sufficient (i.e. your resources are restricted or you aren't using enough of your money), the ability of your Mindful Money Tree to bear fruit is limited. This can occur if your bucket runs out, or if you aren't depleting it sufficiently.

So, once you have identified what fruit you want to grow on your Retirement Tree in the form of your highest values, feed the tree enough to ensure that the optimum level of fruit is grown with just the right level of water and nutrients available in your bucket.

The potting shed

It's in the potting shed that we create the right mix of water and nutrients for your individual tree. The water and nutrients come in the form of financial products, and the shelves of the potting shed are full of them.

The investments shelf is divided into many different sections. You can find ISAs, Open Ended Investment Companies (OEICs), unit trusts, friendly society savings plans, Enterprise Investment Schemes (EISs), Venture Capital Trusts (VCTs), and all manner of investment vehicles. Each section includes subsections, for example in the OEICs section you can find UK equity OEICs, fixed interest OEICs, managed OEICs, OEIC funds of funds, tracker OEICs and so on.

The pensions accumulation shelf is similar. It includes sections for final salary pensions, personal pensions, Additional Voluntary Contribution schemes (AVCs) and Self Invested Personal Pensions (SIPPs) to name but a few. Likewise, in each section there is a subsection of nutrients to choose from. A detailed explanation of all the individual nutrients available is beyond the scope of this book. The point is that there are shelves and shelves of them, and the best mix will be completely individual to you.

You can choose the mix of nutrients to fill your bucket yourself, or you can enlist the support of a professional adviser. The key is knowing what sort of tree you are growing – what type of fruit you want to grow based on what type of life you want to lead.

I am often asked how much pension income other people receive, or what level of life insurance other people have. It is impossible to pick the right mix of nutrients for your tree based on what other people are using. They might be growing an apple tree while you want to grow peaches. What other people have is irrelevant unless they are trying to grow the exact same tree as you, and since no two people are the same, not even identical twins, finding two identical trees would be like finding two identical fingerprints.

CHAPTER 14

Evaluate

In the reconnect component of the RETIRE process we considered what is important to you as an individual, what your highest values are and how these values transcend the six key areas of life represented by the branches of being on your Mindful Money Tree. We are building a picture of the life you want to lead – your 'target'.

Having reconnected with your highest values and set the target, you can move on to the second component in the RETIRE process, evaluate. Evaluating how well established your Mindful Money Tree is currently is the next step towards being able to formulate the right mix of nutrients to cultivate the fruit of fulfilment.

I come from a family of keen orienteers. If you aren't familiar with the concept, orienteering is a sport where you are required to navigate your way through unfamiliar terrain with the aid of a map and a compass. One of the first orienteering lessons my children learned is to make sure they know where they are on their map.

It is impossible to navigate a path to the finish if you don't know where your starting point is. Even if you lose your way en route or obstacles fall in your way, as long as you can work out where you are, you can navigate your way back on track and forge a path to the finish.

Sometimes, finding out where you are can be all you need.

CLIENT STORY
Lisa and John

My first meeting with Lisa and John was in late summer 2014. Lisa had already retired from her successful career as a GP, and John was hoping to be able to retire in two years' time on his 65th birthday. Having worked for a number of different employers in the past, John explained that he had poor pension provision. When John retired, the couple knew they would experience tough times.

They wanted to know from me how bad it was going to be and when John would be able to stop work. They had thought about the cutbacks they were going to need to make and were planning to downsize to a smaller property so that they could supplement their bucket in retirement.

We pulled together a clear picture of their current financial position (more on how below). As a result, we identified that John could in fact afford to retire a year earlier than he had planned, and they could remain in their current home for at least the next 10 years. The simple act of providing clarity over where they stood financially enabled Lisa and John to realise that they didn't need to make many changes at all to live the life they wanted. They were better off than they had anticipated, and by identifying this, they were able to plan to enjoy more of the fulfilling activities that they had previously considered unachievable.

We continue to work together now that they are both retired. My role with them is as much to ensure that their bucket doesn't get too full as it is to ensure it doesn't run out.

Cash flow modelling

A cash flow model, in the context of financial planning, is a method of pulling together all the inflows to and outflows from your bucket. Taking today as your starting point, how do the inflows to your bucket compare with the outflows from your bucket, and how does the value of your bucket change over time?

The best way of illustrating how the cash flow model works is by considering an example.

CLIENT STORY
Jane

I was introduced to Jane by a mutual friend. Approaching her 60th birthday and a recent divorcee, Jane was looking for some guidance on how to structure her finances. She had been left with a lump sum and an investment property from her divorce settlement, but had little in the way of retirement provision. Her husband had been awarded the family home. The small starter home he and Jane had purchased as a buy-to-let investment was now Jane's home.

Jane's primary concerns were what to do with her lump sum and how she would manage financially in retirement. She enjoyed her work and was happy to continue for as long as she was able, but there was a lingering concern that she would not be able to cope financially as and when she needed to cut back or stop work.

We agreed that it would be sensible to use cash flow modelling to build a picture of where Jane stood financially. This is what her 'base plan' cash flow model looked like.

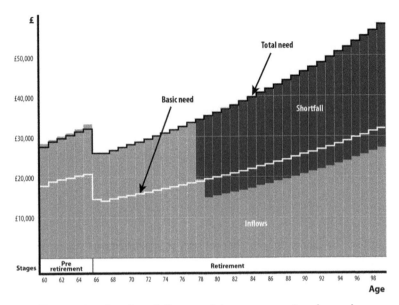

Figure 14.1 - Jane's cash flow model – summary view, base plan

Figure 14.1 sets out Jane's inflows and outflows in each planning year over time. Time is represented on the horizontal axis, and for Jane we chose to model her position until age 100. The bold black line indicates Jane's overall expected expenditure including tax.

When we created the model, Jane's income was slightly in excess of her expected expenditure, which is broken down by basic need (bills and other committed expenditure), represented by the blue line on the chart, and discretionary expenditure (shopping, holidays, leisure pursuits).

The base plan assumes Jane stops work at age 66 when she becomes eligible for her state pension, and her expenditure reduces at that time because she is no longer paying tax on her income. Jane is initially able to use the cash lump sum from her divorce to supplement the income from her state pension and cover her expenditure needs, but by the time she's 78, the cash will run out and she is expected to face an income shortfall, represented by the red in the chart.

The detailed view of the cash flow model (Figure 14.2) demonstrates how Jane's income is made up.

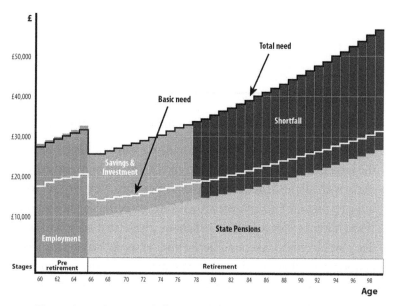

Figure 14.2 - Jane's cash flow model – detailed view, base plan

And we can also view the value of her bucket (i.e. liquid assets) over time (see Figure 14.3).

Your base plan represents where you are now. It includes your expenditure as you would like it to be, not necessarily as it is now. If your bucket can't sustain your desired lifestyle then you want to know about it sooner rather than later so that you can make some adjustments to get to where you want to be.

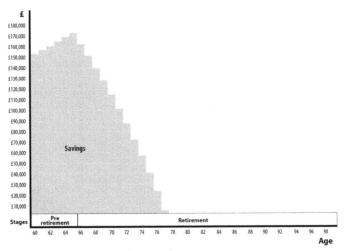

Figure 14.3 - Jane's liquid assets – summary view, base plan

It is necessary to make lots of assumptions when pulling together the base plan. Part of the conundrum is knowing what choices to make with all the ingredients in the potting shed, but don't get too hung up on this. I always recommend erring on the side of caution. If you haven't made a decision yet about what structure you would like your income to take, assume the lowest risk option possible. For pension pots, this would be a scheme pension if your pension is a defined benefit (final salary) pension, or a guaranteed lifetime annuity if your pension is a defined contribution (money purchase) pension.

If you have cash in the bank, assume this is going to stay in the bank for now. Unless you know exactly what you would like to do with it, go for the safest option.

For Jane, the process of pulling together the plan was enlightening. Although the model demonstrated a clear shortfall in later retirement, she was pleasantly surprised that she had enough in her bucket to last her until age 78.

We discussed various different options for extending the life of Jane's bucket. She was comfortable taking some risk with the lump sum she had available to her so we considered a range of different investment options. We crunched the numbers and considered Jane's personal preferences and highest values to devise a plan to restructure her finances, and were able to formulate a plan to extend her bucket by five years.

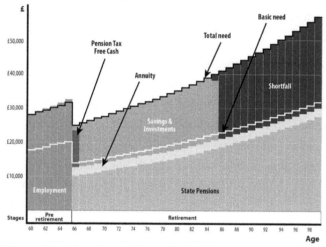

Figure 14.4 - Jane's cash flow – detailed view, proposed plan

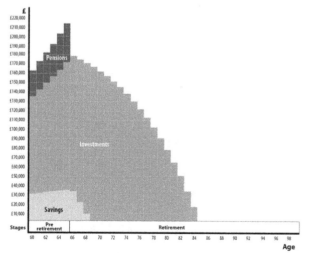

Figure 14.5 - Jane's liquid assets – summary view, proposed plan

Jane has two financially independent sons and it is important to her to leave them something as an inheritance, but she explained that they were likely to inherit from elsewhere. She fully expected to need to diminish the value of her estate to extend the life of the bucket for as long as possible and sustain a comfortable lifestyle during her retirement, and she was happy with this.

We explored the option of releasing equity from Jane's property in the future to provide an income or a lump sum of capital which could supplement her pension income in retirement (see Figures 14.6 and 14.7). Although releasing equity will not be necessary until her bucket runs out, exploring it as an option and understanding its impact was a weight off Jane's mind. She realised that she could top up her bucket and potentially extend it for another 14 years.

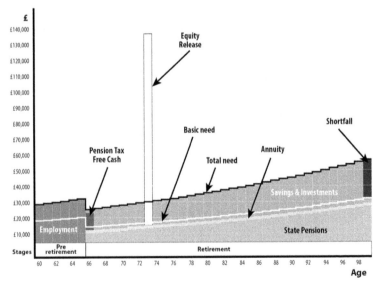

Figure 14.6 - Jane's cash flow – detailed view, proposed plan with equity release

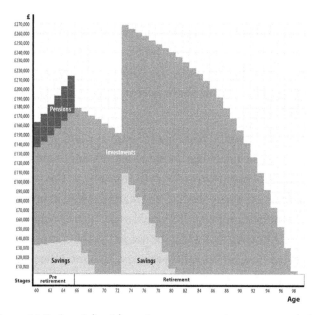

Figure 14.7 - Jane's liquid assets – summary view, proposed plan with equity release

Once Jane felt more comfortable about her financial position, she became willing to think about what a truly fulfilling life would look like and considered options she had never believed possible. She disclosed that she was keen to buy a larger property so that, if her sons had families of their own, she would be able to accommodate grandchildren comfortably and take pleasure in entertaining in her own space. The desire to spend time and create memories with her family during her lifetime was a much stronger motivator for Jane than the thought of leaving them a lump sum of cash on her death.

After we implemented Jane's initial plan, we continued to work together, reviewing her position on a regular basis and revising her goals and ambitions. Around three years after we first met, I was delighted to get a call from Jane asking if she could make a withdrawal from one of her investments to assist with the purchase of a new home. She sold her starter home and purchased a larger property, providing her with the entertaining space and extra bedroom she desired, that she had chosen for the reasons that were important to her.

By withdrawing capital from her investments and upsizing, Jane would reduce the life of her bucket to age 80, but thanks to some strong investment performance in the meantime, this was still an improvement on where she had first started. More importantly, it gave Jane the new property that would make such a positive impact on her life. Knowing that when she needed to, she could still access equity in her now higher value property, Jane took the plunge.

Owning a higher value property would potentially enable Jane to benefit from a higher level of house price growth. A property valued at £250,000 that grows in value by 3% each year will be worth £307,468 in seven years' time. Growth of £57,468. A property valued at £300,000 that grows in value by the same 3% each year will be worth £368,962 in seven years' time. Growth of £68,962.

Of course house price growth at this or any other level is not guaranteed, but as long as growth is positive, owning a larger value asset at the time when her bucket is expected to run out will provide Jane with greater scope to release equity and potentially increase the size of her estate after her death.

Where do you start?

The first and most important step in building the cash flow model is to get to the bottom of what you want your future to look like, what your highest values are and how you would like them to transcend the various aspects of your life. We have covered the importance of identifying our highest values in the previous chapters, and this is the starting point.

We have also started putting numbers on things, making our goals specific and measurable. It is unlikely that you will have all your goals clearly defined prior to putting together a cash flow model. Part of the benefit of putting together the model is that it will refine your thinking. Having a picture of what you would like your life to look like at the outset is useful, but don't worry if some goals or parts aren't clear.

As the model comes together, you will likely come across unexpected choices, identify previously unforeseen possibilities and consider entirely new options. The construction of the cash flow model will, in itself, help you connect with your highest values.

CHAPTER 15

Planning Expenditure

Knowing what you want your future to look like will enable you to estimate what your expenditure will be over time. Your expenditure on regular bills, holidays and one-offs all need to be considered and factored into the model.

Go back to the expenditure analysis you conducted in Chapter 12. As well as providing an insight into your highest values, what you are spending currently is your starting point for the cash flow model.

The next step is to think about how you would like your expenditure to change. For example, if you have identified travel as one of your highest values, make sure you give yourself a big enough travel budget. Do your research; price up the round the world trip of your dreams or the family holiday to Disneyland.

If you want to start singing lessons, get in touch with a singing teacher. Find out what their rates are and factor them in. If you want to buy a place in the country, where will it be and what will it cost? You may want to budget for extra expenditure each and every year, or include one-off expenses at different points in the future.

You can download a free expenditure template at www.retirement-compass.co.uk to prompt you to identify all of your expenditure.

Factor the goals in

Take the goals you began formulating in Chapter 12 and highlight those that need to be taken into account in your financial planning. Make sure you have included them in your spending plan.

By factoring in what you aim to spend in realising your goals, you are well on your way to making those goals a reality. Only 1% of people set goals, write them down and review them. We know that our Reticular Activating System (RAS) will support us in achieving what we believe to be important, so it stands to reason that we are much more likely to achieve our goals if we clearly define them and plan for them to happen.

A study, published in the *British Journal of Health Psychology*, measured how frequently people exercised over a two-week period. People were split into three groups and each group was asked to record how frequently they exercised over the next two weeks.

Members of Group 1 were asked to read the opening three paragraphs of an unrelated novel. **Members of Group 2** were asked to read a leaflet about the benefits of exercise for reducing the risk of heart disease. They were also told that, *'Most young adults who have stuck to a regular exercise program have found it to be very effective in reducing their chances of developing coronary heart disease.'*

Members of Group 3 read the motivational pamphlet and got the same speech as Group 2, but they were also asked to formulate a plan for when and where they would exercise. All members of Group 3 were asked to complete the following statement: 'During the next week, I will partake in at least 20 minutes of vigorous exercise on [day] at [time of day] at/in [place].'

Two weeks later all three groups submitted their exercise records. In Group 1, 38% of participants exercised at least once per week.

In Group 2, the figure was only 35%, but in Group 3, a staggering 91% of participants exercised at least once a week.

By being specific, writing down *when* and *where* they intended to exercise, the participants in Group 3 were much more likely to follow through.

Rocks in a jar

Steven Covery tells the story of a lesson on time management, where a professor produces a large glass jar and places it on the desk at the front of his class. He proceeds to fill the jar with as many large rocks as he can fit in, then he asks the class, 'Is the jar full?'

The students nod and mumble their agreement that the jar is full. The professor then produces a bag of grit and pours it into the jar, filling the gaps around the larger rocks.

'Is the jar full now?' he asks. The class, slightly less sure this time, nod their agreement.

The professor then produces a bag of fine sand and pours that into the jar, filling the remaining space around the rocks and the grit. Finally, he pours a jug of water into the jar until it is full to the brim.

'So what is the message here?' the professor asks his students.

'That no matter how busy you are you can fit more stuff in?' shouts one of the students.

'That if you organise your activities into different types you can fit more in?' suggests another.

'No,' says the professor. 'If you don't put the rocks in first, you will never fit them in.'

Our rocks are those activities that enable us to live our highest values. The first appointments to be entered into my diary each year are our family holidays. Now that you know what your rocks are, make sure you schedule them in before anything else.

Your cash flow model

The figures you put into your spending plan should initially be in today's prices, but you will need to factor in the effect of inflation. Of course, we can only estimate the figures, as it is impossible to know exactly how much your replacement car will cost in three years' time, but give yourself a best guess budget, and always err on the side of caution. When dealing with expenditure, I recommend working on the worst case scenario.

If you think you will spend between £15,000 and £20,000 replacing your car in three years' time, include a figure of £20,000 in your spending plan. We can always work backwards, but if you have under-estimated your budget, you will never achieve what you truly want. If you have over-estimated, you will just end up with more in savings than you had planned for.

Unlike many other expenses, liabilities should have an end date, so I would suggest separating them from expenditure in your model. Loans, mortgages and credit cards as well as any other form of debt should be listed, with details of the amounts outstanding, monthly payments, interest rates applicable and the remaining loan term.

I am a huge fan of Excel spreadsheets and use them for almost everything, but for comprehensive cash flow modelling, a more specialist solution is necessary. There are a number of different software solutions available to assist you and/or your adviser with the process of cash flow modelling. I use a package called

Voyant with clients which I have found to be comprehensive, accurate, visually appealing and relatively easy to use.

Possibly the least exciting part of the process is obtaining and inputting the details of your existing assets into your cash flow model. These are all the financial products, policies and arrangements that are available to provide inflows to your bucket, either now or in the future – pensions from historic employment, state pensions, cash savings, investments, premium bonds and so on.

You can perform the audit process yourself or enlist the support of a professional adviser. You will need to get hold of some up to date information from your existing financial services providers. The exact details you are looking for will differ depending on the type of arrangement you are assessing. With a final salary pension, for example, you will need to know when you will be eligible to receive benefits and how much income you are projected to receive. If you are considering retiring early, identifying the early retirement factors that apply is essential. You may also want to clarify any death benefits.

If you have a money purchase pension, the underlying value of the fund will be important because that will determine what level of income might be available at retirement. Details of any guarantees that apply to your pension plan and the terms under which these apply are key. With some policies, taking benefits early might significantly influence the level of income you can achieve.

For non-pension investments, you will need details to include current values, the underlying investment funds and structure, as well as any surrender penalties.

It is impossible to list everything that needs to be asked because every arrangement and the pertinent factors will differ depending on your circumstances and objectives. A professional adviser will be best placed to ensure that all bases are covered.

State pension. If you do not already have details, you can visit www.gov.uk to obtain a state pension forecast online. Your forecast will identify your entitlement to state pension and tell you when you reach state retirement age.

Income. You will also need details of your current income from employment, self-employment or any other sources.

If you are receiving income from existing assets, for example a pension in payment or an investment property, this income will be entered as well as the asset value itself.

Pulling everything together

Once you have full details of all your existing arrangements, you can enter these into your cash flow plan. Some elements might be quite straightforward. For example, unless you intend to defer it, you know when the state pension is due to be paid and how much you will be entitled to. Defined benefit schemes are also likely to have a fixed retirement date, and a recent statement will provide you with details of your entitlement to income as well as any tax free cash. Although there will be options available to you, I would recommend always going with the lowest risk or default option initially with a view to refining your choices when you come to the 'what if?' analysis.

I have touched upon some of the more technical aspects of retirement planning within this book so that you have an idea of the sorts of things to consider, but it is impossible to cover all the detail here, or to personalise it in any way. You can find further information, guides and articles about specific topics by visiting www.retirement-compass.co.uk.

CHAPTER 16

Translate

Having worked through the concepts and tools that make up the evaluate step in the RETIRE process, you will have your first view of how your inflows and outflows map out over time. The cost of the lifestyle that enables you to connect with your highest values and grow the fruit of fulfilment on your Mindful Money Tree should be factored in.

This initial or base plan will give you a glimpse of where you stand financially and how this compares with where you would like to be. It will highlight any shortfalls and therefore provide you with a better idea of where you need to focus for the next step in the process, translating goals and desires into clear actions.

The best way to guide you through the translate component is with an example cash flow model. Figure 16.1 looks at the base plan for Jim (60) and Cat (63), a couple planning to retire on Jim's 65th birthday.

A good cash flow modelling tool will enable you to see how your income is made up each year, and to what degree you are relying on savings and investments to supplement your more guaranteed forms of income like salary or pensions. As well as modelling your income and outgoings over time, your cash flow model will enable you to see how the value of your bucket changes over time.

The value of Jim and Cat's bucket (their liquid assets) is represented in Figure 16.2.

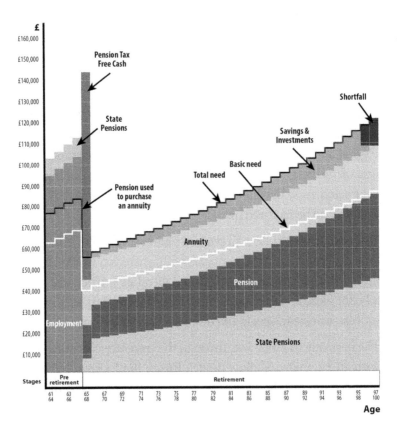

Figure 16.1 - Jim and Cat's Cash Flow
(Detailed View, Base Plan)

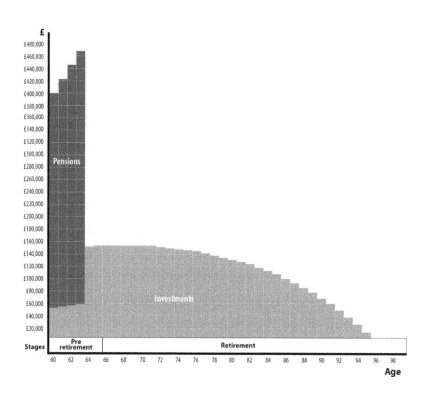

Figure 16.2 - Jim and Cat's Liquid Assets
(Summary View, Base Plan)

The cash flow model predicts that Jim and Cat's pension income will not be sufficient to meet their planned expenditure. They are expected to need to draw on their savings and investment (their bucket or liquid assets) to supplement it. The chart illustrates how their liquid assets are projected to run out completely by the time Jim's aged 95.

As well as shortfalls, you may see an income excess, where the inflows exceed the flow of liquid out of the bucket. If this happens, you will need to think about what action to take with this excess. It could be that you direct it into a specific savings or investment account, or you could choose to assume that you will spend any excesses.

Other applications for the cash flow model

Provided you have gathered and input the right detail about your various existing assets, your model will be able to demonstrate the impact of catastrophic events such as the death of one partner.

Jim was concerned about the impact of his death on Cat, because the majority of their household income was held in his name. Having taken the time to input the appropriate expenditure and income to the model, we can easily identify the impact by running a scenario where Jim passes away two years after retiring.

Figure 16.3 shows that Cat's financial position is significantly affected by Jim's death. Despite her reduced household expenditure, she is projected to be unable to maintain her desired lifestyle beyond the age of 78. At this stage, it is useful to refer back to the assumptions we made at the input stage to identify whether there are any options available to them to improve their situation.

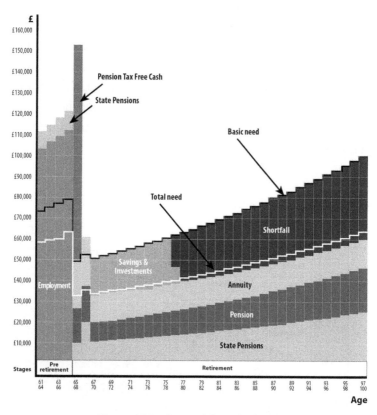

Figure 16.3 - Jim and Cat's Cash Flow
(Detailed View, Jim's Premature Death)

As our default option, we had assumed Jim would convert his defined contribution pension into an annuity, after drawing the maximum 25% tax free cash. We assumed a lifetime annuity which would continue to pay out 50% of the guaranteed amount to Cat in the event of Jim's death. Jim and Cat are comfortable with taking a higher risk approach with Jim's defined contribution pension because he has a level of guaranteed income in place through his final salary scheme and state pension in the future, which will cover the majority of the committed household expenditure. We therefore considered an alternative approach, reflected in Figure 16.4.

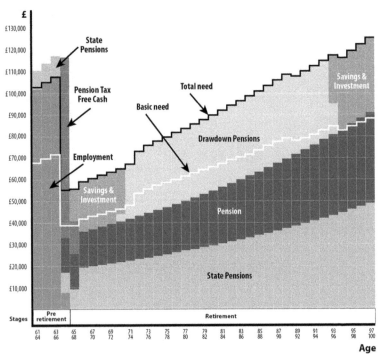

Figure 16.4 - Jim's Early Retirement (Cash Flow, Detailed)

If the couple choose to enter into a drawdown arrangement rather than purchase an annuity, the full value of the defined contribution fund would be available to Cat in the event of Jim's death and she could use this to supplement her income. If we re-model the catastrophe scenario assuming Jim chooses to invest in drawdown rather than an annuity, Cat's financial situation is expected to improve.

If the assumptions we have made hold true, Cat's bucket in the event of Jim's death is extended from age 78 to age 95.

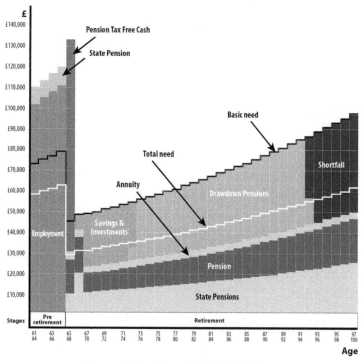

Figure 16.5 - Jim and Cat's Cash Flow
(Detailed View, Jim's Premature Death in Drawdown)

'What if?' scenarios

In addition to considering the impact of catastrophe events, you can use your base plan to model 'what if?' scenarios.

What if Jim were to retire a year earlier? What if Jim were to cut down to a three-day week for the last 18 months?

It is important to start with your goals factored in, and your 'what if?' scenarios should represent possibilities for reducing shortfalls by taking different approaches to organising the flow of liquid into your bucket. This is really where the knowledge and experience of a professional can pay dividends. Unless you know what the possibilities are, you might never even consider them – you don't know what you don't know.

CLIENT STORY
Lynne

Lynne was referred to me by a client I had done some work for a number of years ago. She was recently divorced and had been awarded a share of her ex-husband's pension which was already in payment. Although her ex-husband was receiving a pension from a final salary scheme, Lynne's entitlement would be paid as a lump sum which she was required to invest in a new pension arrangement.

Lynne had always preferred to take a low risk approach to investing. She was aware that she could invest the funds in a drawdown account and draw a regular income or lump sums as required, but she had quickly discounted this option because the risk associated with it was too great.

Lynne initially asked me to conduct some research to identify which pension provider would provide her with the highest annuity in return for the lump sum. This, she felt, was the only option available to her given her wish to avoid any investment risk. She wasn't keen on annuities because she hated to think that, if she were to die in the short term, the full value of the pension would be lost. She didn't really need the income – her other pension income was sufficient to provide her with a comfortable lifestyle, and with her state pension due to be paid in five years' time, her income position would be improved further. But to avoid risk, this was the only route she believed to be possible.

As we chatted in detail about Lynne's goals, aims and values, she disclosed that her real dream was to buy an investment property. Property investment was something she had experience of, and renovating property inspired and motivated her.

We considered the option of drawing the full value of her pension credit as a lump sum, but because Lynne was approaching the higher rate threshold, she would have had to pay a higher rate of income tax on the majority of the lump sum. Effectively she would be giving away 20% of the fund unnecessarily.

I suggested to Lynne that she consider drawing part of the fund as a lump sum in combination with a fixed term annuity, which would enable her to draw more income than would be available from a standard lifetime annuity, over the five years until her state pension became payable. This would enable her to put down a deposit on an investment property and take out a mortgage to fund the rest of the purchase. The income payable from the fixed term annuity would roughly match the level of the state pension and would comfortably cover her regular mortgage payments should the property be untenanted for a period. Although she would pay some higher rate tax on the lump sum drawn, the regular income amount kept her within the basic rate tax threshold going forward.

In addition, at the end of the fixed term annuity in five years, a guaranteed maturity value would be available to Lynne, providing her with a capital pot to either re-invest in another fixed term annuity, draw as a lump sum or convert to a lifetime annuity, depending on her circumstances and requirements at the time. In the meantime, she was able to purchase the investment property she had dreamed of without paying an excess of higher rate tax. The guaranteed maturity value was known at the outset and is not affected by investment returns, thus avoiding any risk.

Lynne would never have considered this option without a conscious identification of the desire to purchase an investment property. Even then, she would not have identified the solution we ultimately put into place, simply because she didn't know that such a solution existed.

It is important that everything is considered in combination and that's the beauty of the cash flow model. You might be willing to take a higher degree of risk with one pot, but only if a second pot is afforded a greater degree of security, so by considering everything in combination, you have the best view.

Actions

Having played around with different 'what if?' scenarios and considered as many possibilities as you can to bridge any shortfalls, you can identify specific actions to achieve the goals you have set for yourself.

For Jim and Cat, the specific actions to come out of the plan are:

Action 1 – Jim to retire one year earlier than planned.

Action 2 – the couple to enter flexi-drawdown arrangements at retirement rather than purchase annuities.

Action 3 – to contribute to an ISA over the next three years while Jim is working to boost their liquid assets in retirement.

The updated cash flow model incorporating these changes is shown in Figure 16.4.

Limitations of cash flow modelling

Your cash flow model can only ever be as accurate as the information you put into it. If you use inaccurate inputs, you will get inaccurate results.

It is always necessary to make some assumptions. For example, you will need to estimate the rate of inflation. Every year, your expenditure is likely to increase with the general rise in the cost of living.

Any capital you have invested, whether it be in defined contribution pensions, investments or cash, will potentially achieve some level of growth. If it is cash in the bank, you will need to make an assumption about the interest rate payable on those savings. If you have invested in the markets, you are less likely to be able to predict what rate of return you might achieve accurately.

Because it is impossible to be accurate about each and every variable being input into the model, it is important that you review your model regularly to refine and update assumptions. This is where the evolve component, covered in Chapter 17, comes in.

Implement, Realise And Evolve

This chapter will cover the three remaining steps in the RETIRE process, the elements probably the most traditionally associated with financial advice or planning. My belief is that traditional financial planning has let us down because it has neglected the first and most fundamental step in the process: reconnecting people with their highest values. Although there are many caring, dedicated and highly intelligent financial planners out there, unless they have a clear understanding of what an individual wants to achieve, they could be crunching the wrong numbers entirely.

By following the first three steps in the RETIRE process – *reconnecting* with your values, *evaluating* your current financial circumstances and how well they support those values, and *translating* your evaluation into clear and meaningful actions – you will have a firm basis from which to put plans into action.

Implement

With your values and intentions clear and your cash flow model drawn up, it's time to put plans into action. This might sound simple, but it is where quite a lot of us fall down. It is easy to put things off until tomorrow, or get distracted by something seemingly more urgent.

The financial services industry doesn't make things any easier. Even after 15 years working in the industry, I find myself baffled by the communications of some financial services providers. I sometimes wonder whether things are designed to make us think they are more complicated than they actually are, and we're silly for not understanding them. If providers baffle us with science then perhaps we won't ask too many questions.

The reality is, even if you call a provider and ask a question, the answer you get might differ depending on which call centre operative you speak to. It is also not unknown for providers to send out erroneous information. A terminally ill client recently received a statement advising him that his wife would be entitled to less than 10% of his pension on his death. Understandably distressed at how this would impact her, he queried this with his pension provider, who eventually acknowledged that in fact she would be entitled to 50% of the pension and the original statement had been issued in error.

Never be afraid to ask questions if communications are unclear. If something doesn't sound right, don't just assume that the financial services provider knows better than you.

Putting theory into practice

The other thing to bear in mind is that what is feasible in theory doesn't always match up with what is possible in reality.

Now that pensions freedom legislation is in place, it is theoretically possible to withdraw the full value of your pension fund as a lump sum or take a flexible income of as much or as little as you like – fantastic. But of course, the reality isn't quite that straightforward.

As we saw earlier, in order for you to access your pension flexibly, it must be a defined contribution (money purchase) pension. If you have a defined benefit pension, flexibility is only available if you transfer out of your current scheme and into a defined contribution arrangement.

If your defined contribution pension is valued at more than £30,000, you will need to take advice from a qualified adviser before making the transfer, and this comes at a cost. Your adviser will need to follow a detailed process of analysis, set out by the Financial Conduct Authority, which takes a significant amount of time and expertise. The transaction will incur a monetary cost for the adviser as it will increase the cost of their professional indemnity insurance, as well as the fees they pay to the regulator.

Even if you have a defined contribution arrangement, your pension provider, or your particular contract, may not facilitate your preferred income structure, so you may find you need to transfer the fund elsewhere before being able to access it flexibly.

As I have said before, it is essential that you ensure you have identified any guarantees or protected funds that apply to your existing arrangement before you transfer because they are likely to be lost on transfer. The other consideration is tax. Any amount you withdraw from your pension, other than the tax free cash element, will be subject to income tax.

Pensions are just one example of how, when you come to the detail, things are often more complex than first meets the eye.

Realise

Once you have successfully implemented your plans, you are well on your way to living the life you want to lead. It is unlikely, however, that you will just wake up one morning and find that you are in a sudden state of euphoria. For a start, many of the plans you put in place now will not have immediate consequences, but just knowing that you have taken positive action to live more in line with your values can provide fulfilment in itself. Whether everything is already in place to support you, or you are still on your journey to having everything in place, the most important thing you can do to achieve the state of flourishing is to be aware, to live in the present moment.

My ambition is to enhance levels of wellbeing in society by using the financial planning process as a mechanism for a more mindful way of living. Approaching life in a mindful way takes practice and I am certainly no master at it, but I recognise the times I achieve it. Sometimes while I am undertaking an activity I enjoy, I feel a sense of fulfilment, contentment and awareness, but I often have to remind myself to change my perspective when this sense is lacking.

A friend and I were discussing what it meant to be mindful. She described how she had been looking after her three-year-old grandson the previous week, an activity she looked forward to which satisfied one of her highest values of supporting and enjoying experiences with her family. They were in the garden sweeping the leaves from the lawn and her grandson was trying his best, but seemed to be making the task ten times harder by regularly dislodging the pile of raked leaves, sending them flying back on to the lawn.

Sensing that she was becoming frustrated at the situation, my friend reminded herself to focus her awareness on spending time with her grandson, not on sweeping the leaves. She described enjoying a sense of calm awareness in focusing her attention on what mattered at that specific moment.

There may be times when we are required to undertake activities that seem pointless, or that we really don't want to have to do.

Our enjoyment of these activities can be improved by considering how they are serving our highest values.

Colin and I recently had some building work done, knocking down the wall between our kitchen and dining room. The work should have taken a couple of weeks and we had put together a makeshift kitchen in another part of the house. Part way through the work, we discovered original flagstones hidden under the tiles and lino. Having spotted them, there was no way we could tile over them, so we took on the not insignificant task of uncovering, lifting, cleaning and relaying them, putting the kitchen out of action for a further six weeks. With no running water in our makeshift kitchen, we had to wash everything up in the small bathroom sink, invariably making the job much harder and more time consuming.

On about week three, I remembered to focus on being more aware of the activity itself – the feel of the warm water, the action of my hands and the varying levels of effort required to remove different marks from the dishes. The sound of the water and the clink of the plates on the ceramic sink. The thoughts of frustration at the extra time it was taking, and that the job had fallen to me yet again. Letting those thoughts be there without judgment; letting them come and go.

Accountability

If this book has motivated you to align your daily activities and personal finances to your highest values, one of the easiest ways of achieving the goals you set for yourself is to share them with someone else.

The chances are, if you are at an age where you are considering retirement, you know others who are doing the same. Whether it is your spouse, a sibling, friend or colleague, I encourage you to speak to others about their values and retirement goals. By sharing your thoughts, you are all the more likely to achieve your goals.

Set up an accountability group where you can share ideas and challenges. Organise a walking group, a photography group, a book club or a computer club. You might find that you have common interests that you can build on. For example, if you are into travel, share holiday photos, destination ideas, hotel reviews and so on. If you want to learn to play the piano, join an online forum for newbie pianists. We all have so much to contribute. Don't fear that you aren't good enough or that others will know better than you. Believe in yourself and get involved.

Evolve

One of my son's school reading books told the tale of two boys who had to help their grandmother who had spotted a thief jumping over her garden wall. The boys rushed out of the house and down the street to the telephone box to call the police.

My son was baffled. 'Why didn't they just phone from their grandma's house?' he asked.

'Not everyone had telephones at home in the olden days,' I replied.

'Okay, so couldn't they use their mobile, then?' was his response.

To a six-year-old, it is unthinkable that instant communication was once not an option. Times change so quickly, and sometimes almost without us noticing. Society changes, and we certainly change as individuals. Our goals, priorities, circumstances and purpose will naturally alter over time. Although our highest values remain relatively consistent, they may change in priority based on our experiences.

Our financial priorities and plans need to adapt over time to ensure they are still serving us as individuals. They also need to adapt to changes in legislation, and to keep pace with industry and product developments.

I would recommend revisiting your Mindful Money Tree at least annually to reconnect with what is truly important to you. Depending on the structure of your financial plans, you may wish to review things more frequently. I have clients with whom I meet on a quarterly basis and others whom I see once a year. Should a dramatic change in circumstances arise, for example the death of a spouse or a divorce, a more comprehensive review is often prompted.

Even if your priorities and purpose are unchanged, you need to review your finances to ensure that they are on track to achieve their targets. Unfortunately, none of us can see the future, so any cash flow model is based on a number of different assumptions. It is essential that we sense check these assumptions on a regular basis and adjust them as necessary. The most appropriate frequency and structure of these more technical reviews will differ depending on how your finances are structured.

For clients who have invested in actively managed portfolios, I typically review the funds making up their portfolio on a six-monthly basis. Based on detailed analysis provided by investment research partners, I recommend tweaks to the underlying funds and allocation of assets to maximise the potential returns within their predetermined risk budget.

For clients who have invested in passive portfolios or funds of funds (see Chapter 7 for an explanation of the different fund types), an annual check-in is likely to be more appropriate because, by its nature, this type of fund requires less intervention.

PART 3

PLANNING CONSIDERATIONS

CHAPTER 18

An Individual Approach

The most critical thing in any financial planning is that it is individual to you. There are countless 'top tips' and generic recommendations available on the web or through magazines offering useful and thought-provoking information, but they can never provide you with the answers that are personal to you.

Everyone is individual, so even if two people had exactly the same cash flow chart and shortfall, the right way to address that shortfall would be different for each depending on their highest values. That's why it is so important to start by reconnecting with your values before you think about the nitty gritty of the finances.

In this chapter I will set out some real life examples of how I have worked with clients to address various planning needs. These examples are designed to help you think about the ways in which you may be able to structure your finances to support your personal values.

If your cash flow chart identifies a shortfall, there are various options available to you to reduce or eliminate it, including reducing outgoings by repaying debt.

CLIENT STORY
Ben

Ben contacted me just before his 60ᵗʰ birthday because he would soon be entitled to draw benefits from one of his pensions and he wanted some advice on how to structure the benefits. He was thinking about transferring the pension from his final salary pension into a defined contribution pot so that he could make use of the pensions flexibility rules and draw a lump sum in excess of the standard 25% to put towards reducing his mortgage.

We conducted a full review of his household finances. Having had children later in life, Ben was still supporting two children at university. He and his wife had recently renovated their extensive manor house, and although they intended to downsize in the future, they wanted to spend some time enjoying it as a family before having to sell. Regular expenditure was therefore tight, and the couple still had a significant mortgage on the property which meant that they were having to dip into savings each month to cover household expenditure.

We identified that the final salary pension Ben was due to receive had particularly attractive guarantees attached to it and was well worth hanging on to. The income it would produce, however, was still well short of covering the shortfall in meeting their expenditure.

Ben explained that he had three other pensions, but he didn't expect to be able to do anything with them because he had selected a retirement age of 65 when he set them up. We identified that these three pensions could in fact be drawn on at any time from the age of 55 onwards without any penalties applying.

The combined value of the three pensions meant that Ben would be able to repay his mortgage in full just with the tax free cash. Once the mortgage was repaid, household income would comfortably cover expenditure and Ben wouldn't need to draw any income from the three pensions until such a time as his wife, 10 years his junior, chose to stop work. Being moderate to high risk by nature and comfortable with accepting an underlying risk to the value of his pension capital, Ben was happy to invest in a drawdown account so as to avoid the need to draw any income at all, while retaining the flexibility to do so should his circumstances dictate.

CLIENT STORY
Lance and Nel

If you have surplus income available to you in the short term, could you be setting this aside to assist with covering a shortfall in the future?

Lance and Nel approached me for advice two years prior to Lance's planned retirement date. Lance was eligible to draw benefits from his employer's pension at the age of 63, but he would need to wait until he was 66 before his state pension became payable. Although the couple were projected to be financially secure once Lance's state pension started, the three-year period between him finishing work and the state pension starting saw them £5,000 a year short of meeting their planned expenditure.

Lance and Nel had some surplus income while Lance was working. By making a few fairly simple cost savings, including negotiating a more competitive tariff for their gas and electricity and reducing their spend on non-essential items, the couple were able to set aside the amount they needed to cover their early retirement shortfall.

Taking risks

Generally speaking, the higher the level of risk you are prepared to take with your investments, the higher the potential return. On the flip side, though, the greater the chance is that the value of your investment will fall.

Figure 18.1 plots the returns of five different investment portfolios ranging from high risk (portfolio A) to low risk (portfolio E) over a year.

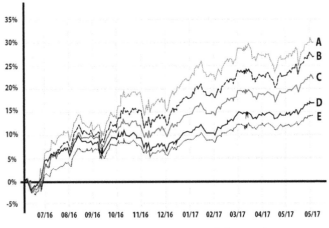

Figure 18.1 - Investment portfolios - risk

As you might expect, the lower risk portfolios experienced lower levels of growth and the higher risk portfolios experienced higher levels of growth. The level of volatility experienced by each portfolio, that is the extent to which the underlying value fluctuated, was much greater in the higher risk portfolios. The performance of the five portfolios in mid-May demonstrates this well.

As we have seen before, if you can afford to wait to ride out any ups and downs, then taking on risk may be more acceptable. However, if you know that you will need to access your capital in the short term, for example to assist a child with a house deposit next year, it would be sensible to adopt a low risk approach to ensure that you have the required capital available whatever happens in the wider markets.

Knowing that with a higher risk approach there comes an increased risk of you ending up with less, you'd be well advised to consider your overall financial position and how any high risk element fits in. If your basic needs are met by more guaranteed forms of income or capital, taking a risk with a small lump sum might be more acceptable. If a drop in the value of your investment will leave you without the income you need to pay your bills each month, taking a high risk approach would not be advisable.

Deferring retirement

Deferring drawing on your pensions might be something you are happy to consider if you enjoy your work and are able to carry on. For every month you defer retirement you are able to contribute more to your pension, and all other things being equal, the older you are when applying for pension income, the lower the cost of providing that income will be.

This is only one option to consider in the context of your higher values. If your primary objective is to be able to stop work, you may prefer to avoid this option at all costs. If, however, you can grow the fruit of fulfilment on your Mindful Money Tree while continuing to work, this might be a welcome solution.

You don't need to stay in your current job to continue working. You could reduce your hours or have a complete change of career.

CLIENT STORY
Jennifer

When I met her, Jennifer was a successful head teacher. Although she had always enjoyed her job, by the age of 60 she had really had enough. The long hours and stress were beginning to take a toll on her health and she was keen to leave the profession a year before she was entitled to draw on her pension.

Jennifer chose to retire from headship but continue working as a consultant on a part-time basis. Although her income dropped significantly, she earnt enough to be able to maintain her comfortable lifestyle while avoiding the need to draw on her pension early. This meant that she avoided early retirement penalties, ensuring her income in the future would be sufficient to sustain her chosen lifestyle indefinitely.

In fact, Jennifer continues to enjoy her part-time consulting work even now that she is drawing her full teacher's pension. She enjoys the challenge of the role and chooses to continue working on her own terms, in the knowledge that she is financially secure without it.

Downsizing

You may have considered downsizing in the future to release a lump sum that you can use to top up your bucket. When we looked at Jane's cash flow analysis in Chapter 14, we saw how releasing equity from her property enabled her to extend the life of her bucket.

CLIENT STORY
Graham and Molly

When they were first introduced, equity release arrangements were extremely expensive and restrictive and attracted a justifiable amount of bad press. I was contacted by Graham and Molly who had unfortunately been stung by an equity release salesman back in 2002.

Graham and Molly had always dreamt of retiring to the seaside, and in making the move and downsizing, they intended to repay their outstanding mortgage. However, when the couple started to make enquiries, they were told that if they did so they would have to give up 25% of the value of their existing home. Their previous adviser had sold them an equity release mortgage without them being fully aware of the consequences, and it was in fact the complete opposite of what they needed. They were still paying regular interest to the lender, but the lender also owned a share of their property. The property had increased in value significantly since they had taken out the mortgage, but

25% of all the growth would be lining the pockets of the equity release company.

The couple were devastated. They were keen to leave an inheritance to their children and they didn't want to give up on their dream of moving to the coast, so they went ahead with the move and repaid the equity release company. It meant that they had to take out a new mortgage and Graham had to continue working for five years longer than the couple had planned to claw back what they had lost as a result of entering the equity release arrangement.

They recalled how their previous adviser had promoted the arrangement as a special limited edition deal. Looking back over the paperwork, we identified that the arrangement had lined his pockets with over £10,000 of commission. Funnily enough, they didn't see him again after he had put the loan in place.

Thankfully, nowadays equity release loans are fully regulated and there are a number of providers competing with each other to provide much more reasonable products. They are still relatively expensive arrangements to enter into, though, particularly if you opt to 'roll up' interest. Rolling up means that instead of paying the interest on a monthly basis, the charge is added to the loan each month. The up side of this is that there is no monthly cost to the borrower. But because the interest is added to the loan amount, you end up paying interest on the interest.

There are now arrangements available that give you the option of covering some or all of the interest charges, which means that you can make sure the amount of the loan does not increase. This can be useful if you wish to protect the value of your estate and you, or a family member, have income available to meet the monthly payments.

CLIENT STORY
Lesley

Lesley approached me because her interest only mortgage was coming to the end of its term and she had no means of repaying the £130,000 balance. She was very happy in her home and didn't wish to move. Even if she had been willing to move, once the mortgage balance had been repaid she would have struggled to find anywhere to live for the money she had available. She was just about able to meet the small interest payment on her current mortgage, but couldn't afford to pay any more. Because of her low income, she didn't qualify for a standard mortgage of anywhere near the amount she would need to repay her existing mortgage lender.

Lesley was keen to maximise the inheritance she would leave to her two sons, but couldn't see how she would be able to achieve this. She put me in touch with her elder son and we chatted through the scenario and the various options. He didn't have a lump sum available to be able to help out his mum, but he did have surplus income each month.

After weighing up the options with her family, Lesley took out a lifetime mortgage on her property to replace her existing loan. Her sons met the monthly interest payments which ensured that the mortgage balance did not increase and therefore their inheritance was protected. If for any reason circumstances changed, the loan could revert to a roll up mortgage so Lesley would not find herself facing monthly mortgage payments she couldn't afford.

Another option available to you if you are faced with an expected shortfall is to cut back on expenditure. It may be that you are willing to do this, but I would recommend thinking carefully about where you intend to cut back and how this might influence your ability to bear fruit on your Mindful Money Tree.

If you value something highly, don't give it up lightly. Even though an alternative solution, for example equity release, might not be ideal, with a clearer idea of what you value most, you can identify whether it is preferable to giving up something else.

CLIENT STORY
Geoff and Carrie

As we have seen in previous chapters, it is not just a shortfall in your bucket that you are trying to avoid. It is equally important to ensure that your bucket is not too full.

Geoff and Carrie spent their working lives setting aside capital for a rainy day. By the time they reached retirement, they had pots of capital all over the place. I first met Carrie following the sad passing of her husband Geoff just after his 87th birthday. She asked to meet with me to discuss how best to invest her savings which Geoff had always managed in the past. She thought she might need to invest them in a higher risk environment in order to achieve higher returns because interest rates were so low and she wasn't entirely sure how much she had or how long it would last.

We chatted through her background and wider financial circumstances and identified that her pension income was more than sufficient to cover her modest outgoings. She had no children and no desire to leave an inheritance. When we got to the bottom of all the accounts, we found that Carrie had over £600,000. She didn't need any of it to cover her living expenses, but she was scared to spend it on things she enjoyed for fear of the pot running out.

I demonstrated to Carrie that she could spend £20,000 a year for the next 30 years without her bucket running out and it was a revelation to her. In fact, if she didn't spend it, on her death 40% of it would be lost in tax.

It wasn't sensible for Carrie to invest any of the capital in anything other than cash based deposits as she simply didn't need to take the risk. I set her the challenge of working out how she was going to spend at least £20,000 a year going forward. While Carrie was excited that she would be able to take holidays with girlfriends and visit new places, her excitement was tinged with sadness that she and Geoff hadn't been able to enjoy some of those experiences together as she now knew that they had had the financial means to do so.

Financial planning isn't just about saving; it is just as much about spending on the right things.

CHAPTER 19

Protecting Your Mindful Money Tree

Identifying and mitigating risks

There are two different types of risk to your Mindful Money Tree: risks that are personal to you, like illness, injury or death, and risks that are external, such as economic factors, investment returns and financial companies going bust (counterparty risk). In order to ensure that your Mindful Money Tree is able to bear fruit even in adverse conditions, identify the various risks that exist and guard against them as best you can.

We face many different risks during the course of our lives, and the most pertinent differ depending on our stage of life, circumstances and family situation as well as our values and goals. While this chapter doesn't provide an exhaustive list, it identifies the risks that are typically more pertinent for those approaching and in retirement.

Death

This is probably the most obvious risk of all because it is the most catastrophic for your loved ones. If you share your bucket with another, for example a spouse or partner, you will want to consider what impact your death will have on your shared bucket and whether it will be adequate to provide the flow of required nutrients after you have gone.

A fundamental aspect of financial planning is considering what you would like your estate to look like, how much you want to leave behind and what form it will take. In addition, you will need to consider how you would like your estate to be distributed. Who gets what and in what proportion?

By writing a will, you can ensure that your money and property, referred to as your estate, are distributed in accordance with your wishes and dealt with by a person of your choice. The person you appoint to carry out the terms of your will is called your executor.

If you die without a will, you are deemed as having died intestate and your estate will be distributed in line with the rules of intestacy.

There is a useful guide to who is entitled to a share of someone's money if they die without making a will at www.gov.uk/inherits-someone-dies-without-will. For some people the outcome may be acceptable, for others it may not. The process will also generally take longer if you die intestate.

Inheritance tax

Inheritance tax is a hugely complex area of financial planning. This section aims to summarise the key points and highlight issues it is useful to be aware of, to research or discuss in more detail with your professional advisers should it be appropriate.

If the value of your estate on death exceeds the inheritance tax nil rate band, then the excess will be taxed. The nil rate band at the time of writing is £325,000 for each individual, and anything over that amount is subject to tax at 40%. If you are married, any unused nil rate band can be transferred to the surviving spouse on the first partner's death.

Gifts to charities are free of inheritance tax, and certain other assets, such as businesses, woodland property, heritage assets and agricultural property, benefit from exemptions, allowances or reliefs.

Some gifts you make while you are alive may be subject to inheritance tax. In summary:

- Each individual has a £3,000 gift allowance each year, so a married couple can gift £6,000 between them. You can give away cash or assets up to this value without incurring any inheritance tax

- You can carry over any unused gift allowance from one tax year to the next, up to a maximum of £6,000

- Any outright gifts made in excess of the gift allowance are known as 'potentially exempt transfers'. Provided the person making the gift survives for seven years there is no tax to pay

- If the person making the gift dies within seven years of making it, the value of the gift may be subject to inheritance tax

- The tax due may be reduced by taper relief – the older the gift, the lower the rate of tax

- Gifts that are made into certain trusts may attract an immediate tax charge, as well as a 10-yearly anniversary charge.

In addition to the £3,000 gift allowance, certain other gifts are always tax free, including:

- Gifts between husband and wife or civil partners

- Gifts made as part of 'normal expenditure'. To qualify as tax free, gifts would need to be from surplus income rather than capital. A good test of whether a gift is from income is whether it comes from a current account rather than a savings account and can be made without adversely affecting the donor's standard of living

- Gifts to people getting married. Each parent can gift up to £5,000 to a child, and a grandparent, or other relative, can gift up to £2,500. Non-relations can gift up to £1,000

- Gifts of up to £250 per recipient. These gifts are meant to cover Christmas and birthday gifts.

New rules are being phased in that will mean each individual can qualify for an additional threshold (i.e. extension to their nil rate band) if they are passing on their home to a child or grandchild. This additional threshold is the lesser of the value of the individual's share in the property, after any mortgages have been repaid, and the maximum additional threshold amount on the date of death. For deaths in the following tax years, the maximum additional threshold will be:

- £100,000 in 2017–2018
- £125,000 in 2018–2019
- £150,000 in 2019–2020
- £175,000 in 2020–2021.

Any unused additional threshold can be transferred to a surviving spouse, and an estate may also be entitled to an additional threshold when an individual has downsized to a less valuable home, sold or given away their home since July 2015. Where an estate exceeds £2,000,000, the additional threshold will be gradually tapered away.

Inheritance tax planning may well have an important part to play in ensuring that your personal finances are truly aligned to your values. However, remember to keep those values at the core rather than being directed down a certain path in pursuit of tax savings at the expense of all else.

Power of attorney

A lasting power of attorney (LPA) is a legal document that lets you (the 'donor') appoint one or more people (known as 'attorneys') to help you make decisions, or to make decisions on your behalf should you have an accident or an illness that results in you being unable to make decisions at the time they need to be made.

There are two types of LPA. **Health and welfare** gives the attorney the power to make decisions about things like your daily routine, medical care and moving into a home. **Property and financial affairs** gives the attorney the power to make decisions about money and property for you, for example managing your bank accounts, selling your home or paying bills. You can choose to make one type of LPA or both. A health and welfare LPA can only be used when you are unable to make your own decisions, but a property and financial affairs LPA can be used as soon as it is registered, with your permission.

We often associate LPAs with older individuals who are perhaps suffering from dementia and therefore unable to make decisions for themselves. This is probably the most common time when an LPA is needed, but it can be needed at any time and at any age.

A will writing colleague described how one of his clients did not have an LPA in place and suffered a life changing skiing accident at the age of 45. He was unable to manage his own affairs due to the extensive brain injuries he suffered and, without an LPA in place, his family did not have the authority to deal with his affairs. It was necessary to undertake a lengthy process of applying to the court for a deputy to be appointed. In the meantime, with nobody able to look after it, the client's business couldn't continue to function, pay its liabilities or provide his family with its regular income. Had this particular client put an LPA in place, his attorney would have been able to take over the running of the company immediately to ensure that it was able to continue functioning and supporting him and his family.

External risks

Investment risks. We touched on investment risk in the preceding chapters. The level of risk it is appropriate to take varies depending on many different factors.

Knowing what your plan is and how you want your money to serve you and support your values is the first key factor. If you are considering investing a sum of money for a specific purpose, you are much more likely to be able to make the best decisions.

Being clear about why you are investing might be more difficult than it sounds. I have lost count of the number of times I have asked clients about the purpose of their investment and they have looked at me somewhat blankly. Knowing why you are making the investment, or considering the range of possibilities for using the capital in the future if there is more than one possibility (which is fine), enables you to identify the following.

Investment timeframe. The longer the period of time an investment is made over, the less impact short term value fluctuations are likely to have.

Andrew and his wife Jenny are renting a house temporarily, having sold their previous home. They have bought a brand new energy efficient home off plan and it will be completed in six months' time. The new, larger property will accommodate their growing family at Christmas and other get togethers.

The proceeds of the sale of the previous house are sitting in the bank earning zero interest. Andrew saw himself as a high risk individual and was keen to invest the capital for the maximum return possible to boost the size of the pot.

Figure 19.1 - Returns of a high risk portfolio

If Andrew had invested in the high risk portfolio modelled in Figure 19.1 in September 2008, when he came to draw the money in March 2009, its value would have dropped by 30%. Andrew wouldn't have had sufficient to cover the cost of the house he had committed to buying and he would have been forced to take out a mortgage on the property to meet his obligations to the developer.

If you know that you are going to need to draw on capital within three to five years, it is sensible to keep that capital in a lower risk environment, even if it means accepting a lower return.

Your personal risk profile. All of us are unique. Some people enjoy the thrill of taking risks while others shy away from it. If taking a risk with your investment is going to keep you up at night then don't do it.

CLIENT STORY
Kerry and Dan

Kerry and Dan had secured lucrative contracts overseas and were earning five times the amount they needed to cover their living expenses. They had invested the excess in a high risk investment linked savings plan. They were keen to secure the maximum growth possible and were both comfortable with risk, having taken it on numerous occasions in the past.

All was going well until the credit crunch hit in 2008. The value of their investment plummeted from £150,000 to £75,000 almost overnight. The couple called me in a blind panic, saying, 'Sell, sell, we've lost everything.' I convinced them to hang tight, which they did for a day. The value fell further and they pulled out of their investment, realising a loss of over £80,000 on the value their portfolio had been less than a week previously.

If they had kept hold of their investment it would have bounced back. In fewer than six months the value would have been above where it had been before the crash.

Market timing is the strategy of buying or selling financial assets by attempting to predict future market price movements. Typically, investors trying to time the market fail. They buy too late and sell too early, missing out on the most significant growth and realising the biggest losses. Identifying what you want your investment to do for you, investing it in an appropriate risk environment and holding a position for the long term is the most advisable course of action, but it must be a position you feel comfortable with. Even if markets appear to be falling to records lows, taking your investment with them, you need to be comfortable with sitting on your hands and avoiding the urge to cash out.

If you can't face the thought of the value of your investment falling by more than a certain amount then limit the risk you are taking with it. If it is set up correctly in the first place, you shouldn't need to cash out during times of uncertainty. Even if you are comfortable with risk, it is important to consider whether you have the capacity to take it.

Bert and Tim are brothers who have each inherited £200,000 following the death of their great aunt. They would both like to invest the £200,000 to top up their income in retirement. They completed a risk profiling questionnaire and scored four out of five on the risk scale – moderate to adventurous.

Both Bert and Tim require an income of £15,000 pa to cover their regular expenditure. Bert has a final salary pension from his previous employer which provides him with a guaranteed income of £20,000. Although he doesn't need additional income, he would like to be able to have the option of taking longer holidays each year and would welcome a bit more flexibility in regular spending.

The state pension is Tim's only source of pension income. He receives £9,000 each year and has been working to generate income that will meet the rest of his expenditure, but his health is deteriorating and he would like to be able to stop work and replace his employment income with income from his inherited lump sum.

The impact of a dramatic fall in value would have a more significant impact on Tim than it would on Bert. At worst, Bert would need to cut back on discretionary expenditure, but he would still have a comfortable standard of living. A dramatic fall in the value of Tim's investment might result in him being unable to draw the income he needs to cover his committed outgoings.

Before taking any risk, think carefully about what the impact of a fall in the value of your investment would have on your standard of living. Could you comfortably sit tight and wait for the value to rise again or would you find yourself unable to live your chosen lifestyle? Also think carefully about whether you need to take risk. You may be comfortable taking risks, but if you don't need to then it may be sensible to avoid doing so.

For example, Carrie, whom we met in Chapter 18, was prepared to take a higher degree of risk than she was currently taking. A risk profiling questionnaire put her at a two out of five on the risk scale (cautious to moderate). However, she had absolutely no need to do anything other than let the cash sit in the bank earning minimal interest. She would never spend it all and she had no desire to leave it behind so it would be pointless for her to take extra risk, and incur extra cost, unnecessarily.

Counterparty risk. *Mary Poppins* was one of my favourite films as a child. I remember the scene where Mr Banks is in a state of high anxiety as everyone is pounding down the doors of the bank, trying to withdraw all their money. To me it was complete fiction, part of a wonderful story. I didn't even consider that it could really happen in modern day society, but it was that scene that sprang to mind when in 2007, I turned on the news to hear about the run on Northern Rock. It did actually happen; it is possible for a bank to go bust.

Thankfully for Northern Rock savers, and those savers with NatWest and RBS who were also bailed out, the UK Government was able to ensure that nobody lost their savings. It might not be the same story next time, particularly now that it has happened once, so it is wise to ensure that your savings and investments are protected by the Financial Services Compensation Scheme (FSCS).

The protection limits change from time to time and can be found at www.fscs.gov.uk. Cash deposits with banks and building societies are currently protected up to £85,000 per person per institution. It is important to check which institution your bank or building society is protected under because many individual financial services brands actually fall under the same institution. For example, Halifax, Bank of Scotland and BM Solutions are all part of the HBOS group, and only £85,000 per person will be protected across the whole group.

CHAPTER 20

Summary

Welcome to the Mindful Finance Movement! Now you have read this far, I hope that you are eager to put the tools I have outlined to work in aligning your personal finances with your true highest values and structuring them to support the retirement that is a reflection of you.

Your relationship with your finances can be depicted by the Mindful Money Tree. Your identity is the trunk, which extends to experience the world through the six branches of being. Each branch enables you to grow the fruit of fulfilment, and you will need to engage with each different element to identify the form your individual fruit takes.

Your money comes in the form of the liquid and nutrients from your bucket, absorbed by the tree through the root system and necessary to grow the fruit, but it is not the fruit itself. The root system filters your financial interactions by your past experiences and beliefs around money.

Mindful Finance in retirement

The word 'retirement' is outdated. It traditionally meant stopping work and living a quiet life, but we now use the term in a much broader context. It could mean reducing hours, changing career, or continuing in your current role. Perhaps a more appropriate term to describe the transition we are discussing in this book is the decumulation shift – the transition from building up your assets to drawing on them to support you in living your chosen lifestyle.

The RETIRE process has been devised to assist you in applying the concept of Mindful Finance in retirement. It is worth reflecting on the six key components of the RETIRE methodology. This chapter acts as a quick reference guide, summarising the individual elements of the process and listing the tools and exercises that will assist you in each step.

Reconnect. Our intrinsic highest values, those things that give us our own unique identity, are often lost in the pursuit of society's ideals. If you get nothing else from it, I hope that this book has helped you to reconnect with your highest values. This is the first step in being able to consider how you can align your finances to a retirement that inspires and fulfils you.

How do your past experiences around money and the money messages taught to you by your parents influence your perspective on your finances? List at least five specific goals for living in retirement, and give each goal a number, for each of the six branches of being:

- Vitality

- Attachments

- Lifelong learning

- Universe and environment

- Enjoyment

- Significance.

What are the common themes? Are your goals interrelated and do they appear to be supporting similar values? Where are you spending your money? Which values are you supporting?

Reflect on your answers to George Kinder's three questions, particularly question three. Then list your three to five highest values.

Evaluate. In the evaluation component your aim is to build a clear picture of where you currently stand financially, what the inflows to your bucket are, how they balance with the outflows and whether your bucket will be sufficient to sustain the life you want to lead. Equally important is to consider whether your bucket is becoming too full. What is the greater evil – outliving your resources or living an unfulfilled life?

Map specific and measurable goals in the form of planned expenditure into your plan. Factor in that round the world trip or your early retirement. Your Reticular Activating System will help you get what you plan for.

Translate. When you've identified where you want to be and where you stand now, discover what actions need to be taken to achieve the retirement you desire. Considering the range of options available to you for structuring your finances in the context of your highest values will enable you to refine the myriad of options to identify those that best serve you.

Run 'what if?' scenarios on your base plan. For example, 'What if I retire early?' or 'What if I work another year? What if I buy the house of my dreams? What if I double my holiday budget?'

Consider the impact of catastrophe scenarios such as illness or death. How would this impact on you or your loved ones?

List the specific actions you will take to achieve the life you desire.

Implement. All your efforts to this point are worth little if you don't put your plans into action. This can be made more difficult than it should be by the complexity and jargon adopted by financial services providers. Don't be put off. Unless you see your plans through, you will not realise your dreams.

Don't be afraid to ask questions. If something isn't clear, ask for an explanation. Get to the bottom of the practicalities. Check with your existing financial services providers that your specific contract enables you to take the action you are planning.

Realise. If you formulate plans and then put them into action, you might think you will achieve fulfilment automatically. What is important is being aware that you are realising your goals, and that can take work. Take the time to be truly present in your everyday actions.

If you don't already practise it, give mindfulness meditation a go (I recommend www.headspace.com).

Evolve. Change is inevitable, and it is important to ensure that your plan remains on track into retirement and beyond. Schedule a review of your goals and objectives in your diary. How well does your daily life reflect your ideal day, week or year? How well does your actual expenditure hold up against your expectations? Which assumptions need to be adjusted in your cash flow model?

Making the transition to retirement isn't easy. It can be daunting, confusing and pretty scary. I hope that this book has provided you with a starting point for reducing the complexity, clarifying what is important, and taking the action required to transform your relationship with your personal finances so that they deliver the retirement *you* want to lead.

Acknowledgements

Writing this book is a huge personal milestone for me and I would like to thank the many people that have made it possible.

In particular, I thank my mum and dad, my husband Colin and my two children Martha and Freddie for supporting me in their individual ways.

A huge thank you to all the clients I have had the pleasure of working with for sharing their journeys with me.

Special thanks to...

The team at Dent Global for giving me the encouragement and belief to write this book, and my 'KPI Dream Team' Heidi Strickland-Clark, James White, Julia Kendrick, Michael Anderson and James Herbertson for holding me accountable.

My test readers Debbie Shipcott, Anne Piper and Brian Darch for your time, encouragement and constructive feedback.

Lucy, Joe and the team at Rethink Press for providing the structure, process and guidance to make my ambition a reality.

About The Author

Over the past 15 years Emily Macpherson has pursued a quest to combine the power of her analytical brain with her passion for making a real difference to people's lives.

After achieving a first class degree in business from the University of Bath she started her career at a large consultancy as a trainee actuary. It didn't take long before she realised that the corporate world was not for her. Following a negative experience on the receiving end of a financial adviser's 'sales' process, she chose to train as an Independent Financial Adviser, determined to change the way financial advice was delivered.

Emily founded Find Peace of Mind at age 22 and, now a fellow of the Personal Finance Society, has gained unique insights in to her client's relationships with their money as well as the wider problems they face. In this book, she draws on those insights, to present a new way of thinking about personal finance.

As a business owner, mother of two, and active supporter of local community projects, Emily is well aware of the intricacies of balancing time, money and passion to lead a fulfilling life. The purpose of her company is to enhance levels of wellbeing in society by aligning personal finance with personal values and her structured methodology provides those approaching retirement with a clear, purposeful and prosperous way of living.

You can get in touch with Emily at:
www.findpeaceofmind.co.uk
❶ @FPofM
❷ FPoMltd